Changing Times

at the Rocky Mountain
Forest & Range
Experiment Station

Station History from 1976 to 1997

R. H. Hamre

Rocky Mountain Research Station
Forest Service, U.S. Department of Agriculture

USDA Forest Service
General Technical Report RMRS-GTR-146

February, 2005

Abstract

Changing Times includes a review of early Station history, touches on changing societal perspectives and how things are now done differently, how the Station has changed physically and organizationally, technology transfer, a sampling of major characters, how some Station research has been applied, and a timeline of significant and/or interesting events. It includes references to a number of significant publications, and a listing of all personnel from 1976 through 1997.

About the Author

Bob Hamre came to the Rocky Mountain Station from the Forest Products Laboratory in September 1962 as Station Editor. He continued under various titles, including Leader of the Research Information Group, until June 1993. He was Acting Station Director for 1 day. He has digested and edited Forest Service research publications – and written about them – for nearly 50 years, although at a more relaxed pace as a retiree for the past 11 years. He graduated from the University of Wisconsin with a B.S. degree in chemistry in 1952 and an M.S. degree in technical journalism in 1957. He has five professional children, four daughters and a son.

Author's Personal Note: In several places in this document, I have mentioned some of the people who have contributed to the character of the Rocky Mountain Station. Every employee has contributed, but I couldn't include every name. Most of those named are now retired. To all my friends and colleagues who remain un-named, I apologize.

Front Cover Photos (clockwise from top left): 1) water samples from the Glacier Lakes Ecosystem Experiments Site in southern Wyoming help scientists evaluate the effects of pollutants on aquatic resources; 2) studying bald eagle habitat in the southwestern U.S.; 3) evapotranspiration (loss of moisture from needles) studies on the Fraser Experimental Forest in Colorado analyze the amount of water used by the forest overstory; 4) scientists in Bottineau, North Dakota, conduct greenhouse experiments to find trees best suited for planting in the harsh environments of the Great Plains.

Changing Times

at the
Rocky Mountain Forest and Range Experiment Station

Station History from 1976 to 1997

R. H. Hamre (retired)

The Rocky Mountain Research Station is headquartered in Fort Collins, Colorado, in cooperation with Colorado State University.

Station Directors (1975-1997)

David Herrick (1975-1980)

Charles Loveless (1980-1989)

Hank Montrey (1989-1992)

Denver Burns (1992-2000)

Preface

In 1976, Raymond Price, a former director of the Rocky Mountain Forest and Range Experiment Station, chronicled the early history of the Station. Included in that document, General Technical Report RM-27 (see *A Few Significant Publications*, near the end of this history update, for availability), was the history of one of its major early precursors, the Southwest Forest and Range Experiment Station. Ray had also been director of the old Southwest Station before the two were merged in 1953. Scientists and technicians at both of these original Stations contributed generously to the rich knowledge base about forest and range resources in the Rocky Mountains, Great Plains, and Southwest.

With the merger of the Rocky Mountain and Intermountain Research Stations in 1997, a new entity was formed: the Rocky Mountain Research Station. This update of the Rocky Mountain Station history, and a planned history of the Intermountain Station up until 1997, will bring together these two branches that will become the new "tree of research" hailed by Raphael Zon on the outskirts of Flagstaff, Arizona, in 1908. It will be the task of some future historian to chronicle how this new organization melded its talents and physical resources to respond to the information needs of a sophisticated, ecologically aware society, and the technical needs of wildland managers faced with increasingly complex decisions about how that society can integrate uses of those resources.

Table of Contents

A Quick Review of Early History

Research in the U.S. Forest Service was born in the West – the Southwest, to be more precise. Former Station Director Ray Price's original history of the Rocky Mountain Forest and Range Experiment Station (RM Station hereafter) retells the story leading up to Raphael Zon's cry in 1908, "Here we will plant the tree of research!" That seedling of Forest Service research, planted near Flagstaff, AZ – the Fort Valley Experiment Station – grew to become the Southwest Forest and Range Experiment Station, and matured into the RM Station.

The RM Station territory also nurtured the birth of range research with the establishment of the Santa Rita Experimental Range south of Tucson, AZ, in 1903, and of watershed research with the first paired watershed experiment in the United States at Wagon Wheel Gap Watershed in southwestern Colorado in 1910.

The Fremont Experiment Station, established in 1909 west of Colorado Springs, CO, paralleled the Fort Valley Experiment Station. The Fremont supported forest management efforts in the Forest Service's Rocky Mountain Region (R2), while the Fort Valley supported work in the Southwestern Region (R3). These early stations were typically low-budget operations with few, but highly dedicated, investigators. Gus Pearson in Arizona and Carlos Gates in Colorado left indelible tracks for subsequent researchers to follow, started trails that led to fields of research they might only have dreamed about.

With increasing recognition of the importance of National Forests – and of how little we really knew about managing them – Congress passed the McSweeney-McNary Act in 1928, authorizing the establishment of 12 regional forest experiment stations.

Santa Rita Experimental Range, 1915.

Thus funds were appropriated in 1930 for establishing the full-fledged Southwest Forest and Range Experiment Station in Tucson, AZ, and in 1935 for the RM Station in Fort Collins, CO. Forest Service policy was to establish research facilities in close cooperation with State universities, so the SW Station was originally located on the campus of the University of Arizona, and the RM Station at Colorado A&M, which later became Colorado State University.

Fort Valley Experimental Forest headquarters, 1930.

Research on shelterbeds (then popularly called windbreaks) at Lincoln was in direct response to the Dust Bowl conditions of the mid 1930s.

Reorganization within the U.S. Department of Agriculture in 1953 led to consolidation of forest insect and disease research into the Forest Service Research organization. Also in 1953, the SW and RM Stations were consolidated, with Ray Price moving from Tucson to lead the new Rocky Mountain Forest and Range Experiment Station in Fort Collins. To administer a broader, more comprehensive program, the Station's research was organized on a Research Center basis. As Director Price put it, this system had "…several marked advantages: (1) because scientists resided within the areas, they became more intimately acquainted with the people and the problems needing attention; and (2) the people within the areas had a greater opportunity to take part in the programs." Price had an unusual knack for public involvement and political savvy.

Rapid growth of forestry research programs nationwide in the 1950s led to an 8-year boom in the construction of facilities. The Forest Research Laboratory at Rapid City, SD, in 1960 was followed by the Forestry Sciences Laboratory at Flagstaff, AZ, and the Forest, Range, and Watershed Laboratory at Laramie, WY, in 1963. The Forest Hydrology Laboratory at Tempe, AZ, was dedicated in late 1965, and the Station's new Headquarters/ Office/Laboratory complex in Fort Collins in summer 1967. The Forestry Sciences Laboratory at Lincoln, NE, was completed in 1968. The Shelterbelt Laboratory in Bottineau, ND, (built in 1963) became part of the RM Station in 1966.

The 1950s also saw an evolution from Research Centers to laboratories with Project Leaders directing specific areas of research, such as watershed, silviculture, and range.

Growth of the research program subsequently led to a 1965 restructuring of how Station research was organized and administered. The results were four major areas of research, each headed by an Assistant Director, under Ray Price, Director:

- Forest Economics, Utilization, and Recreation Research   R.D. Lloyd
- Range Management and Wildlife Habitat Research   E.H. Reid
- Timber Management and Forest Protection Research   G.L. Hayes
- Watershed Management Research   H.C. Fletcher

All supporting technical and administrative services were coordinated under the heading of Station Management, led by D.M. Ilch.

As environmental aspects of wildland management and research moved to the fore in the early 1970s, a national trend toward multifunctional research work units developed. These consolidations and reorientations led to Servicewide reorganizations of Experiment Station structure in 1973, with a more geographic approach:

Director:
Karl Wenger
Deputy Director:
David Herrick
Assistant Director for Continuing Research, South:
Vincent Duval
Assistant Director for Continuing Research, North:
William Laycock
Assistant Director for Planning and Application:
Harold Paulsen
Assistant Director for Research Support Services:
Donald Morton

The ADR South, stationed in Tempe, had responsibility for research in New Mexico, Arizona, and western Texas; the ADR North, stationed in Fort Collins, had responsibility for research in North and South Dakota, Wyoming, Colorado, Nebraska, and Kansas.

Ray Price was right on target, as usual, when he closed his summary of RM Station history with this observation: "As 1975 drew to a close, the theme of the Eisenhower Consortium sponsored symposium at Vail, Colorado in September, *'Man, Leisure, and Wildlands: A Complex Interaction'* might well set the course of forestry research in the central and southern Rocky Mountain Region in the years ahead."

In October 1975, the RM Station staff totaled 220 full-time employees: 90 Project Leaders and scientists, 50 technicians, 74 research support and technical, and 6 Director's immediate staff. For early "grey literature" on the history of Forest Service research in the Rocky Mountain region, see the unpublished reports footnoted below.

1   Roeser, J. Jr. 1955. A brief chronological history of the Rocky Mountain Experiment Station.(Typewritten report, Apr. 18, 1955, on file, library, Rocky Mountain Forest and Range Experiment Station, Fort Collins, CO.
    Storey, H.C. 1975. History of Forest Service research: Development of a national program. (A working report, Apr. 24, 1975, on file at USDA Forest Service, Washington, D.C.)

Organization of the Rocky Mountain Forest and Range Experiment Station, after Consolidation, 1954

DIRECTOR'S OFFICE
Director   Raymond Price
Divisions of Research
  Timber Management
    J. H. Buell, Chief
  Forest Diseases
    L. S. Gill, Chief
  Forest Insects
    N. D. Wygant, Chief
  Forest Utilization
    L. A. Mueller, Chief
    E. S. Kotok
  Range Management
    E. H. Reid, Chief
  Watershed Management
    M. D. Hoover, Chief
Soils Investigations
  J. L. Retzer
RESEARCH CENTERS
Arizona
  Fort Valley, Flagstaff
    E. M. Gaines, Leader
    Timber Managament
      E. M. Gaines
      F. R. Herman
      E. C. Martin
    Range Management
      J. F. Arnold
  Santa Rita, Tucson
    H. G. Reynolds, Leader
    Range Management
      H. G. Reynolds
      J. W. Bohning
      Cooperating ARS
        H. M. Hull
        M. E. Roach
  Sierra Ancha, Tempe
    H. C. Fletcher, Leader
    Watershed Management
      H. C. Fletcher
      L. R. Rich
      D. R. Cable
      Cooperating ARS
        F. Lavin
Colorado
  Continental Divide, Fort Collins
    B. C. Goodell, Leader
    Timber Management
      R. R. Alexander
    Watershed Management
      B. C. Goodell
  Front Range, Fort Collins
    L. D. Love, Leader
    Range Management
      W. M. Johnson

Cooperating ARS
  G. E. Klipple
Watershed Management
  L. D. Love
  Upper Colorado, Delta
    G. T. Turner, Leader
    Range Management
      G. T. Turner
    Watershed Management
      H. E. Brown
Nebraska
  Prairie Research Project, Lincoln
    R. A. Read, Leader
    Timber Management
      R. A. Read
New Mexico
  Upper Rio Grande, Albuquerque
    E. J. Dortignac, Leader
    Fire
      A. W. Lindenmuth, Jr.
    Range Management
      H. A. Paulsen, Jr.
    Watershed Managament
      E. J. Dortignac
      E. H. Palpant
Wyoming
  Big Horn, Laramie
    R. M. Hurd, Leader
    Range Management
      R. M. Hurd
      F. W. Pond
FOREST INSECT AND DISEASE LABORATORIES
Albuquerque, New Mexico
  J. W. Bongberg, in charge
  Forest Diseases
    S. R. Andrews
    F. G. Hawksworth
    T. E. Hinds
  Forest Insects
    J. W. Bongberg
    R. K. Bennett
Fort Collins, Colorado
  B. H. Wilford, in charge
  Forest Diseases
    R. W. Davidson
  Forest Insects
    B. H. Wilford
    C. L. Massey
    W. F. Bailey
    A. E. Landgraf
    R. H. Nagel
    F. B. Knight
    F. M. Yasinski

Projects, Project Leaders, Scientists, and Locations, 1962

ARIZONA

Flagstaff

Evaluation of Watershed Programs
D. P. Worley, Project Leader
- H. E. Brown
- W. P. Clary
- A. R. Tiedemann
- P. F. Ffolliott

Fire Use
- A. W. Lindenmuth, Jr., Project Leader
- J. R. Davis

Management   Woodland and Forest Ranges
- D. A. Jameson, Project Leader
- H. A. Pearson

Silviculture   Ponderosa Pine
- G. N. Schubert, Project Leader
- M. M. Larson
- L. J. Heidmann
- E. C. Martin

Tempe

Management   Chaparral Ranges
- F. W. Pond, Project Leader
- H. D. Chadwick (attached to Albuquerque)

Management   Riparian and Wet Sites
- J. S. Horton, Project Leader
- J. P. Decker
- C. J. Campbell

Water Yield Improvement   Chaparral
- G. E. Glendening, Project Leader
- P. A. Ingebo
- C. P. Pase
- C. M. Skau

Water Yield Improvement   Pine-Fir
- L. R. Rich, Project Leader
- P. T. Koshi

Wildlife Habitat
- H. G. Reynolds, Project Leader

Tucson

Management   Semidesert Ranges
- S. C. Martin, Project Leader
- D. R. Cable

COLORADO

Fort Collins: (*indicates acted as Project Leader in addition to Division Chief responsibilities)

Forest Diseases
Diseases   Montane and Subalpine Species
- F. G. Hawksworth, Project Leader
- J. M. Staley
- T. E. Hinds

Forest Economics
Forest Survey
- R. L. Miller
Market Development Opportunities
- J. M. Hughes, Project Leader
Forest Recreation
- L. D. Love, Project Leader

Forest Insects
Biology, Ecology, and Control of Bark Beetles and Defoliators in the Central Rocky Mountains
- N. D. Wygant, Project Leader*
- W. F. McCambridge
- R. H. Nagel
- M. E. McKnight

Timber Management
Mensuration
- C. A. Myers, Project Leader
Silviculture   Spruce-Fir and Lodgepole Pine
- R. R. Alexander, Project Leader
- F. Ronco
Silviculture   Mixed Conifers and Aspen
- G. L. Hayes, Project Leader*
- J. R. Jones

Range Management and Wildlife Habitat
Forest Biometry
M. J. Morris, Project Leader
Forest Game and Fish Habitat
Dwight R. Smith, Project Leader
Management   Mountain Ranges
H. A. Paulsen, Jr., Project Leader
P. O. Currie
G. L. Spain
Watershed Management
Alpine Snow and Avalanches
M. Martinelli, Jr., Project Leader
A. Judson
Water Yield Improvement; Runoff and Erosion
M. D. Hoover, Project Leader*
R. H. Swanson
J. D. Bergen
B. H. Heede
E. C. Frank
Cooperative Watershed Management Research Unit
B. C. Goodell, Project Leader

NEBRASKA
Lincoln
Diseases   Shelterbelts and Nurseries
G. W. Peterson, Project Leader
Silviculture   Windbreaks
R. A. Read, Project Leader
D. H. Sander
D. F. Van Haverbeke

NEW MEXICO
Albuquerque
Diseases   Ponderosa Pine and Associated Species
P. C. Lightle, Project Leader
J. W. Riffle

Insects   Biology, Ecology, and Control of Bark
Beetles and Defoliators in the Southwest
C. L. Massey, Project Leader
M. J. Stelzer
J. F. Chansler
Range Improvement and Management of Seeded
Ranges
H. W. Springfield, Project Leader
Watershed Rehabilitation—
E. F. Aldon, Project Leader
W. C. Hickey
Water Yield Improvement
H. L. Gary, Project Leader

SOUTH DAKOTA
Rapid City
Forest Utilization (Black Hills)
E. F. Landt, Project Leader
V. P. Yerkes
Silviculture—Ponderosa Pine (Black Hills)
C. E. Boldt, Project Leader
J. L. Van Deusen
Water Yield Improvement (Black Hills)
H. K. Orr, Project Leader
M. L. Geiger
Wildlife Habitat (Black Hills)
D. R. Dietz, Project Leader

WYOMING
Laramie
Management   Alpine and Subalpine Ranges
W. M. Johnson, Project Leader
Dixie R. Smith
Water Yield Improvement   Sagebrush Lands
H. W. Berndt, Project Leader
R. D. Tabler
B. A. Hutchinson

Project Leader's meeting, March 1975, Fort Collins, CO.
First row, seated on ground, left to right: *D. R. Carder, F. G. Hawksworth, R. E. Stevens, G. D. Lewis, R. W. Tinus, D. R. Patton, J. W. Lancaster.* **Second row, seated:** *D. R. Keefer, H. A. Paulsen, Jr., D. A. Lingwood, D. E. Herrick, W. C. Morris, M. B. Dickerman (WO), K. F. Wenger, W. J. Lucas (R 2), W. D. Hurst (R 3), R. Lindmark (INT), W. A. Laycock, V. L. Duvall.* **Third row, standing:** *C. A. Myers, A. J. Bjugstad, A. L. Ward, C. Feddema, H. K. Orr, R. S. Boster, D. D. Elser, G. H. Schubert, H. E. Worth, E. F. Aldon, J. L. Kovner.* **Fourth row, all remaining standing:** *G. W. Peterson, M. Martinelli, Jr., J. F. Thilenius, D. F. Fan Haverbeke, S. C. Martin, R. S. Driscoll, D. G. Fox, W. P. Clary, S. S. Saackett, J. R. Thompson, B. L. Driver, J. H. Dieterich, R. R. Alexander, R. A. Read, R. H. Hamre, R. D. Tabler, L. L. Manley.*

Societal Perspectives Have Changed

How society perceives the nation's forests – and especially how various special-interest groups express their views – has changed dramatically in the past quarter century. In his Foreword to Ray Price's 1975 history of the RM Station, Director Dave Herrick alluded to research that helped forest managers "get much more from timber, range, wildlife, water, and recreation resources than was possible in earlier years," and how scientists are seeking answers to "long-term challenges associated with forest regeneration, improving growth and yield, and protecting forests from insects, diseases, and fires." Foresters were being taught

how to "bring wildlands under management." But societal concerns over clearcutting in the Appalachians and Northwest were making headlines in the nation's newspapers.

Suddenly, or so it seemed, the spotted owl flew out of the "ancient forests" of the Pacific Northwest and into the national limelight. Old-growth forests and natural ecosystems became the battlegrounds of an intelligent, well-informed, ecologically aware – and litigious – public. Forest management in the West was no longer the tightly held domain of professional foresters and those with economic interest in wildland resources. Multiple use

was no longer the quick answer to conflicting demands on forest resources. Even Smokey Bear retreated into near hibernation after the Greater Yellowstone Fires of 1988 brought widespread awareness of fire as an integral part of many natural forest ecosystems.

Against this backdrop of enlightened public awareness and involvement, both forest management and research had to evolve quickly to remain relevant. Where earlier research tended to be more resource-specific – silvicultural treatments to increase timber volume, vegetation management to increase water yields, better grazing systems – the new paradigm was to develop multi-functional research to understand the processes involved in maintaining healthy, dynamic ecosystems. Research would be synergized by having scientists from different disciplines working together. How people fit into the resource management picture became a significant element in the research equation. Chief F. Dale Robertson attempted to institutionalize this more ecosystem-friendly philosophy through his four-point "New Perspectives" initiative: *Sustaining ecosystems, integrating science and management, making flexible responses to resource challenges, and enhancing partnerships with people.*

Director Herrick became a leader in encouraging scientists to form multi-disciplinary teams to address emerging issues. The Station's contribution to the national SEAM (Surface Environment and Mining) program to restore mineland spoils in the Four Corners area and Wyoming, and the Beaver Creek project along the Mogollon Rim south of Flagstaff are prominent examples.

The trend toward multidisciplinary research and quicker application of research findings was further encouraged by changes in Washington that eased resource-oriented budget restrictions. According to Dixie Smith, Deputy Station Director at the time, these fiscal changes in Washington "didn't really change what we were already trying to do, but they certainly made budgeting

the Station a whole lot easier!" Designing effective, multifunctional research work units with broad missions and problem statements would not be easy, however – a situation anticipated by Smith who said, "Defining meaningful problems and ensuring they were translated into tactical research were daunting tasks, with minimal reward to the scientists."

As Director Hank Montrey (1989-1992) put it in a keynote address in Flagstaff celebrating the 100th anniversary of the Forest Reserve Act, "We must obviously move from the functional, single-resource, single-scientist focus on physical and biological sciences aimed at advancing science in a discipline. We need to move toward inter-disciplinary, multi-resource integrated teams that include social scientists. Managers are

faced with the dilemma of making major resource decisions without all the information they would like from either research or the public….Resolving this dilemma is going to require that we all better understand:

- The basic nature of the complex ecosystems we are entrusted with,
- How to protect and conserve the biodiversity in those ecosystems,
- How to deal with conflicting societal demands for resource outputs, and
- How to keep all those balls in the air without impairing the ability of the land to meet the demands of future generations!"

Participants in a 1985 team-building session.
Front row: *Glenn Peterson, Clyde Fasick, Bob Alexander, Glen Brink, Martha Pforr, Debbie Schofield, Charlie Loveless, Harold Coley, Norma Bath, Dick Tinus.*
Second row: *Tom Hoekstra, Earl Aldon, Dixie Smith, Doug Fox, Bob Hamre, Ardell Bjugstad, Rudy King, Debbie Allen, Bev Perotin, Frank Hawksworth, Ron Tabler.* **Third row:** *Jerry Oncken (consultant), Frank Ronco, Marty Raphael, Leonard DeBano, Hans Schreuder, Clarence Adair, Dave Patton, George Peterson, Ed Wicker, Sam Krammes, Dick Gillespie (consultant).*

The Rocky Mountain Station
Has Changed in Many Ways

The Rocky Mountain Station in early 1997 was a very different place from what it was in 1975, physically, socially, and organizationally.

The research staff project leaders, scientists, technicians, and directorate had declined by nearly a third, from 146 to 105 (16, 56, 29, and 4, respectively). The support and technical staff increased from 74 to 86, but this total includes an indeterminate number of people intermingled in the colocation of the Arapaho-Roosevelt National Forest mentioned below.

Karen Burr, Flagstaff, examines the roots of Douglas-fir seedlings grown in "Tinus" book planters after exposure in mist boxes.

Another obvious difference is the role of women in research. When Ray Price referred to "the distaff side," the role of women at the Station in 1975, he meant the wives of scientists, and the secretaries. The three exceptions were Geraldine Peterson (statistician), Mona Nickerson (editor), and Frances Barney (librarian). All three were exceptional they had to be to

reach professional status. When Denver Burns became Director in 1992, Marcia Patton-Mallory was Assistant Director for Planning and Applications, and there was one female Project Leader: Michele Schoeneberger at Lincoln. By 1997 Karen Clancy at Flagstaff, Debbie Finch at Albuquerque, and Linda Joyce at Fort Collins had joined Schoeneberger as Project Leaders, and Patton-Mallory was Assistant Director for Research. Susan Evans (Janzen), Adminstrative Services, Shari Blakey, Personnel, and Angela Chavez, Computer Services, were Group Leaders in Administration. *(In 2004, Marcia Patton-Mallory is Station Director; 2 of 5 Assistant Directors, 5 of 7 Group Leaders, and 7 of 29 project leaders of the new RMRS are women.)*

The physical presence of the RM Station in the field shrank significantly due to decreasing budgets and increasing personnel costs. What had been the headquarters of the old Southwest Station on Tumamoc Hill in Tucson closed in 1978. The Shelterbelt Laboratory in Bottineau was ceded to North Dakota State University in 1982. A recently opened wildlife project at Texas Tech in Lubbock closed in 1983. The Santa Rita Experimental Range south of Tucson went to the University of Arizona as part of a complex land swap involving the State of Arizona, the USDI Bureau

of Land Management, and the USDI Fish and Wildlife Service. The Forest Hydrology Laboratory at Tempe was transferred to Arizona State University as part of a complex arrangement that saw a consolidation of Station research in Arizona to Flagstaff.

Through a lease arrangement, the arid land research unit moved out of downtown Albuquerque into a well-designed laboratory near the airport. Wildlife and archaeological research were added in later years.

A significant addition to the Station was a major new facility in Flagstaff. As part of the deal where the Tempe laboratory on the ASU campus was to be sacrificed to provide space for a new Goldwater Science and Engineering Building (which was eventually redesigned and built *around* the lab) a cooperative arrangement was authorized by Congress with Northern Arizona University. The result was the $20 million Southwest Forest Sciences Complex housing the Station and the NAU School of Forestry. This impressive facility was dedicated in May 1993.

When Dick Krebill transferred to the Intermountain Station in 1982, the position of Assistant Director for Research South was moved from Tempe to Fort Collins.

In March 1983, the Arapaho-Roosevelt National Forest physically colocated with the Station in the headquarters building

A day in the life of a wildlife biologist: Teryl Grubb, Tempe, rappels down a cliff to evaluate a bald eagle nest along the Verde River on the Tonto National Forest, AZ.

on Prospect Road. The driving force for the colocation was the concept of "shared services": tight budget dollars could be stretched if duplicative administrative functions such as personnel, purchasing, etc. were consolidated for the two units. Space was a problem, of course, and several projects and support units were shuffled to the Craddock Building, on the east side of Fort Collins.

During the 1970s and 80s, the Station leadership worked hard and successfully to strengthen research ties with the universities within its territory, and improve cooperation with National Forest Systems and State and Private Forestry units within the Forest Service.

The Eisenhower Consortium for Environmental Forestry Research was established at RM in 1971, with Gordon Lewis as Program Manager, to foster cooperative research among Station scientists and nine universities within the Station's territory: Universities of Wyoming, Colorado, Arizona and New Mexico; Colorado, Arizona, and New Mexico State Universities; Northern Arizona University; and Texas Tech. It was disbanded 10 years later.

How the Station was organized to do research also changed. In the early 1990s, Forest Service Research in Washington instigated a Servicewide effort to promote a strategic planning process at each Station that would emphasize multidisciplinary research along with the more traditional "functional" research. The '90s then saw increased emphasis on building research work units with interdisciplinary teams of scientists focusing on multifaceted problems facing resource managers. Three area-specific "ecosystem management" RWUs were established in 1994: Achieving Ecosystem Management in the Borderlands of the Southwestern United States Through a Coordinated Research/Management Partnership (Carl Edminster, Team Leader); Watershed Processes, Riparian Zone Responses, and Biological Diversity of the Rio Grande Basin (Debbie Finch, Team Leader); and Sustaining Social, Biological, and Physical Components of Colorado Front Range Ecosystems (Brian Kent, Team Leader).

Advantages, according to Director Burns, included:
- Synergy of scientists from different disciplines, universities and management attacking complex issues, rather than individuals looking at pieces of problems.
- Larger units with fewer Project Leaders, with concomitant savings in paperwork and travel.
- Limited money and people resources focused more on problems of public resource management, and less on personal disciplinary interests.

The primary disadvantages were reduced disciplinary breadth and capacity at the Station, particularly in range research and forest health research.

In a significant program expansion, the Station established the Center for Semiarid Agroforestry subsequently renamed the National Agroforestry Center (NAC) in 1992 at the Station's Forestry Science Laboratory in Lincoln, NE, with Bill Rietveld as Center Director. The Center began as a Forest Service partnership between Research and State and Private Forestry, and was expanded to include the Natural Resources Conservation Service in 1995. The NAC conducts research on how to design and install vegatated plantings riparian buffers to protect water quality, and develops and delivers technology on a broad suite of agroforestry practices. The partnership draws upon Forest Service expertise with forestry and trees and harnesses it to NRCS expertise in agriculture and its technology delivery system to farmers, ranchers, and communities. Agroforestry technologies can be readily incorporated into most farm and ranch operations, and provide cost-effective ways to diversify production and increase income, while simultaneously enhancing natural resource conservation.

Stream Team members measure bedload movement on E. St. Louis Creek on the Fraser Experimental Forest.

Also in 1992, the *National Stream Systems Technology Center* was established at the Rocky Mountain Station, with Larry Schmidt as Program Manager. "The Stream Team," as it is better known, was chartered to provide the technology to help forest managers, hydrologists, and fisheries biologists maintain favorable stream flow conditions from the National Forests. Emphasis is on instream flow, channel maintenance and streamside vegetation, and watershed condition. Primary focus areas are on improving knowledge of stream hydrology and related watershed processes, developing operational tools for

managers, providing training and operational support, and identifying research needs. Stream Team findings are applied nationwide by a multitude of governmental and private organizations.

Responding to concerns that the U.S. Department of Agriculture had too many small units to maintain effective public service, the Forest Service began a quest to streamline many operations, including the number of regional Experiment Stations. First to merge were the Southeastern and Southern Stations, with headquarters established in Asheville, NC. Then, in the spring 1992, Chief Dale Robertson directed Hank Montrey and Northeastern Forest Experiment Station Director Denver Burns to informally analyze and report to him on the feasibility, benefits, and costs of merging the Intermountain and Rocky Mountain Stations. Based on their analysis, Chief Robertson set the stage for the merger. In the fall 1992, Montrey transferred to the Forest Service headquarters in Washington D.C., and Burns became the Director of the Rocky Mountain Station.

From 1993 on, increasing emphasis on scientists obtaining "soft money" accomplished three things, according to Burns:
- Incoming money focused research on key problems.
- The ongoing loss of staff was reversed.
- The world's research community became more aware of the high quality and capability of Rocky Mountain Station scientists.

In 1993, Burns was named Acting Director of the Intermountain Station in addition to his responsibilities at Rocky Mountain. A drastic recision of appropriated dollars halfway through fiscal 1995 and major budget cuts in 1996 not only frustrated a joint Management Team, but stressed personnel of the two Stations, already worried about consolidation of locations, programs, and services. During those difficult years, Burns focused considerable energy on a three-pronged effort to ensure that the new Rocky Mountain Research Station would be efficient, effective, and an enjoyable place to work by:
- Integrating both research and administrative support managers from the two Stations into a seamless decisionmaking team.
- Keeping scientists and support personnel informed about, and involved in, working out the details of the consolidation process.
- Involving all four of the National Forest System Regions in the combined Station territory in defining problems and prioritizing research efforts.

After 4 years, during which the entire organization of the Forest Service was proposed for change and change again, the consolidation of the Rocky Mountain and Intermountain Stations was officially approved by the Secretary of Agriculture on May 4, 1997.

Focus of the Experimental Forests Has Changed, Too

The *Fraser Experimental Forest*, established in 1937 on the Arapaho National Forest as a representative site for studying the alpine/subalpine environment of the Central Rockies, can still be recognized from high-flying jets by its herringbone pattern of timber harvests. Research was designed to evaluate effects of tree removal in lodgepole pine and Engelmann spruce forests on snow accumulation and subsequent water yield. Marvin Hoover and Bob Alexander were critical scientists involved. Those harvesting effects are still being evaluated, but most new research addresses questions that deal with broader aspects of hydrologic systems and forest, landscape, and biological diversity processes that better define ecosystem function.

The first watershed study on the Fraser Experimental Forest involved the paired Fool Creek (treated) and East St. Louis Creek (control) watersheds.

The main lodge, like several other buildings at Manitou Experimental Forest headquarters, was constructed by the Work Projects Administration (WPA), and is now on the National Register of Historic Places.

The lower elevation *Manitou Experimental Forest*, established in 1936 on the Pike National Forest, is best known for early research to evaluate grazing systems and range management in the ponderosa pine type. Wally Johnson and Pat Currie were driving forces. Ongoing research is focused on gaining a better understanding of ponderosa pine ecosystems, and the disturbance regimes active within them (insects, disease, fire). Because it has extensive residential in-holdings, and is located near the highly populated Front Range, the Manitou is also uniquely suited for studies of ways to best manage these forests in the wildland-urban interface (WUI).

GLEES, the *Glacier Lakes Ecosystem Experiments Site* on the Medicine Bow National Forest in southern Wyoming, is the Station's newest major study area, though not a formally established experimental forest. GLEES was established in 1987 to conduct long-term integrated studies on the influence of atmospheric deposition and climate change on sensitive alpine aquatic and terrestrial ecosystems. Doug Fox was instrumental in its establishment, and designing integrated research to evaluate the impact of air quality changes on wilderness.

The *Santa Rita Experimental Range*, established in 1903 on Bureau of Land Management lands adjacent to the Coconino National Forest in southern Arizona, was ceded to the State of

A Management Team meeting at Rio Rico in southern Arizona, 1987, included a field trip to the Santa Rita Experimental Range. **Left to right, back row:** Bob Alexander, Charlie Loveless, Bill North, Dave Sturgis, Martha Pforr, Ardell Bjugstad, Len DeBano, Steve McDonald, Marty Raphael, Earl Aldon, Glen Brink, Clark Martin, Terry Shaw, Dick Tinus, Larry Allen, Doug Fox, Clarence Adair, Harold Coley, Hans Schreuder, Bill Kruse, Glenn Peterson. **Front row:** Bob Hamre, Rudy King, Kieth Severson, Ed Wicker.

Arizona in 1990 as part of the complex land exchange that led to the move of the Tempe lab to Flagstaff. As stipulated in the land exchange, the University of Arizona now manages the Range for experimental purposes. The Station is no longer in charge, but scientists do have input into the research program. Clark Martin and Dwight Cable were long-time scientists on the Santa Rita.

As of 1997, only one stream gauging station was collecting long-term hydrologic data on the *Sierra Ancha Experimental Forest* on the Tonto National Forest in central Arizona. The Sierra Ancha, established in 1932, was a primary site for major studies to determine how the interrelated influences of climate and soils, topography and geology, and the nature, condition, and use of watershed vegetation might affect streamflow, soil erosion, floods, and sedimentation from sites ranging from desert shrub to mixed-conifer forests.

Although the original watershed studies were closed in 1983, part of the facility has been used as an ecological study area by Arizona State University through a cooperative agreement. Marvin Hoover, Ron Hibbert, and Len DeBano were among the scientists involved.

Len DeBano and others put considerable effort into developing the *Battle Flat Chaparral Experimental Watersheds* on the Prescott National Forest in Arizona in the 1980s. Weirs were installed on paired watersheds and baseline data collected, but budget reductions resulted in the area being assigned to the Prescott for further development and monitoring.

Fort Valley Experimental Forest, the first Forest Service research forest in the nation, was established in 1908 northwest of Flagstaff. The site was selected because ponderosa pine did not appear to be regenerating sufficiently. However, in 1919, a heavy seed crop followed by a wet spring with no summer drought   a rare event   appeared to solve the problem. For the 80 years since, and in the absence of fire, silviculturists have been studying how to deal with the huge 1919 seedling crop. There were other problems to be solved, however, and Gus Pearson and Gil Schubert published monumental works on the silviculture of southwestern ponderosa pine, centered on research at Fort Valley. Frank Ronco led an effort to sustain research and upgrade facilities in the early 1980s, including stress physiology research, and Dick Tinus's greenhouses, used to develop and apply findings on containerized tree

Vegetation was treated in the 1950s and 1960s on Workman Creek, Sierra Ancha Experimental Forest, in a study to evaluate possibilities for increasing water yields in Arizona.

seedling work. Those efforts have now been completed, or moved to the new Forestry Sciences Complex on the Northern Arizona University campus.

The *Long Valley Experimental Forest* southwest of Flagstaff was established in 1936 as a counterpart to Fort Valley because it is on soils derived from sandstone/limestone, as opposed to Fort Valley's basalt. A rangewide provenance planting of ponderosa pine and some fire-effects research were still active in 1997.

The *White Mountain Watersheds* were set up in eastern Arizona in the late 1950s to determine if results from Workman Creek on the Sierra Ancha could be confirmed and transferred to other mixed-conifer forest areas. Three pairs of experimental watersheds were instrumented: Castle Creek East and West Forks, Willow Creek East and West Forks, and Thomas

Alden (Ron) Hibbert, Tempe, checks an analog-to-digital (ADR) streamflow recorder on the Battle Flat Watersheds, AZ, 1980.

Creek North and South Forks. Treatments were developed that would benefit timber production, wildlife habitat, and streamflow. Thomas Creek was designed to evaluate our knowledge of integrated resource management. The Station transferred monitoring responsibilities for Castle and Willow Creeks to the Apache-Sitgreaves National Forest in 1983, and for Thomas Creek in 1986.

The *Beaver Creek Watersheds* south of Flagstaff were established in the late 1950s to evaluate vegetation management programs designed to increase water yields and other multiple resource benefits in the ponderosa pine forests and pinyon-juniper woodlands of the Salt-Verde River Basin. Scientists under Dave Worley, Ross Carder, and Dave

Garrett measured the impacts of various timber harvest intensities and pinyon-juniper removal on streamflow, soil erosion and sediment production, water quality, timber yield, scenic beauty, and dynamics of wildlife populations. Ecological simulation models were also designed and tested. Beaver Creek was designated as one of UNESCO's Biosphere Reserves in 1976. Information collected at Beaver Creek has resulted in nearly 700 publications in 24 subject areas (see the Baker and Ffolliott annotated bibliography in *A Few Significant Publications*).

Long-term silvicultural research continues on the *Black Hills Experimental Forest*, designated in 1961 near the center of the Black Hills National Forest in South Dakota, but that research is now directed from Fort Collins, along with Black Hills forest health studies. Rangeland/ grassland and wildlife habitat studies continue out of the Rapid City laboratory.

Flood flow after a rain-on-snow event at the flume on Woods Canyon, Beaver Creek Experimental Watershed, AZ, 1978. Ponderosa pine had been harvested at various levels to evaluate effects on streamflow and water yields.

The *Coon Creek Study Area* was established in the early 1980s on the Medicine Bow National Forest near the Colorado/Wyoming border as the site for the Coon Creek Water Yield Augmentation Project. The objective was to evaluate how water-yield increases after operational-scale timber harvesting would compare with increases measured during research-scale studies such as those on Fool and Deadhorse Creeks on the Fraser Experimental Forest. Effects of timber harvest patterns on wildlife, and increased stream flow on fisheries, are also part of the research program. Chuck Troendle was the principal scientist involved in planning Coon Creek. Marty Raphael and Len Ruggiero established major wildlife habitat studies.

The *Denbigh Experimental Forest* in North Dakota was established in 1931, during the Dust Bowl days, to evaluate tree species and seed sources for shelterbelt plantings in the harsh environment of the northern Great Plains. No studies are currently active, and in 1997 the Denbigh was in the process of being decommissioned and returned to the Custer National Forest.

The *Hastings Tract* near Hastings, NE, acquired by the Station in 1968, has been devoted to long-term tree improvement provenance and progeny plantations. Designed primarily by Ralph Reed for shelterbelt research, they are now important sources of germplasm for tree improvement, biotechnology, and biological control research. The Tract, however, is being transferred to the Nebraska National Forests.

Then and Now

Rocky Mountain Station headquarters was a spirited place to work in the late 1970s. Budgets were comparatively good, programs were expanding, and there was a strong feeling of "family." In Fort Collins, an elected Social and Courtesy Committee assessed annual dues, sent flowers when someone was in the hospital, and organized summer picnics and Christmas parties. Everyone from Directors and Division Chiefs to scientists, technicians, and secretaries converged on the "Break Room" for a few minutes mid-morning and mid-afternoon to discuss everything from budgets and research to football scores and their kids' accomplishments. Coffee was an excuse to socialize. But times change, and the Station changed with them. The Social and Courtesy Committee is no more. People walk into the Break Room for a cup of coffee, then go back to their offices to drink while scanning a computer screen. This trend is not a reflection on the headquarters, the Station, or the Forest Service, but on a more hectic pace of life everywhere. Social aspects of the workplace seem to be a declining phenomenon, giving way to everyone being too busy.

And we do things differently now. Project secretaries no longer type and retype manuscripts, making an occasional erasure and correction on four carbon copies. Today, PCs and spellcheck are the way. Scientists create their own manuscripts on personal computers. Visual Information Specialist Pete Cunningham no longer drafts black-and-white charts on a drawing board. What the scientist can't build on the computer, Illustrator Joyce VanDeWater creates in full color images and multiple media with powerful software. Field data aren't laboriously tabulated on punch-cards for analysis on a huge computer a few blocks away on the CSU campus. Technicians key data into small recorders hung on a neck strap as they work in the field. Scientists or their technicians then download recorded data directly into PCs for analysis in minutes in the comfort of their offices. Where scientists previously had to develop their own analysis programs in Fortran, the evolution of readily available software and computer hardware has led to more powerful, faster analyses. And technicians may be graduate ecologists, plant physiologists, or electrical engineers. Phone calls don't go through an operator at the switchboard, and voice mail has replaced the little yellow note describing a missed call. Typed letters and speed memos were replaced by FLIPS, then the Forest Service's Data General computer terminal, then by IBM equipment tied to the Internet. Communication is faster and easier technically but transferring ideas to others is still a challenge and still requires face to face discussion.

That's cool! John Rinne, Flagstaff, seines for spikedace fish on Arizona's Gila River.

Technology Transfer is Still a Challenge

The job of doing research is never really complete until the new knowledge is put to use, not just once, or locally, or even nationally. Over the decades the Rocky Mountain Station has wrestled with the concept of technology transfer: how to get results put to use and applied across the broadest spectrum of disciplines.

The standard measure of a scientist's productivity — the publication — is only a starting point. Getting new technology into the hands — and minds — of potential users is a continuing challenge. Time constraints, lack of personnel, resistance to change, organizational inertia — the roadblocks are many, and the rewards to the scientist for time spent on "TT" are perceived by many as insignificant.

In addition to standard Research Papers, General Technical Reports, Research Notes, USDA Handbooks, Technical Bulletins, and so forth, Station scientists have sought out well over 100 peer-reviewed technical, scientific, applied, and popular journals as recognized quality outlets for their research. The Station generates *New Publications* (www.fs.fed.us/run/main/pubs/newpubs.html), a quarterly list announcing those reports and articles, and mails it worldwide to requesting members of the general public, academia, State and Federal natural resource agencies, and to the District

Ranger level throughout Forest Service Regions in the Station's territory.

But the investment in research warrants more than just announcing new publications, and mailing them free of charge to those who take the initiative to request them. The Rocky Mountain Station aggressively tackled the problem in a variety of ways during the 1976 – 1997 period. Its scientists are well-known for supporting field managers and decisionmakers. However, numerous ways to put science and technology in application have come and gone.

Forestry Research West

In1976, Rick Fletcher came to the Station from Region 3 as a Public Affairs Officer. One of his primary duties was to write articles popularizing current Station research for *Forestry Research West*, a short, quarterly magazine cooperatively published by the Pacific Northwest, Pacific Southwest, Intermountain, and Rocky Mountain Stations. Distributed widely to field locations throughout the Forest Service in the West (and to other agencies and academia), its goal was to alert resource specialists to new research that might help them be better professionals. Rick subsequently became senior editor, responsible for coordinating the writing and publishing of FRW. FRW has since given way to

RMRScience, a quarterly science newsletter (www.fs.fed.us/rm/main/rmrs_reports/index.html).

Symposia

Frustration with the delays of journal publishing, and a growing need for focused attention on specific topics, coupled with the advent of manuscripts submitted by authors in a camera-ready format suitable for publication, led to a sharp increase in the popularity of the symposium as a means of rapid technology transfer. Instructions for authors on how to prepare camera-ready manuscripts developed by Editors Mona Nickerson and Bob Hamre were adopted Servicewide. Because proceedings were typically off the press within 2 months of the symposium, Rocky Mountain Station scientists were actively sought to take the lead in organizing symposia on pressing topics. Close to 50 significant symposium proceedings were published at the Rocky Mountain Station from the mid 70's through the mid 90's on topics ranging from birds and fish to fire history, accuracy of remote sensing, and management of riparian ecosystems.

FS INFO

FS INFO was the final Service-wide step in the evolution of a package of library services that began with CALFORNET at the Pacific Southwest Station in Berkeley. The package included a monthly *Alert* identifying significant published articles and reports in the various natural resource fields in the world literature, *delivery of documents* requested from these Alerts, and *individualized literature searches* of worldwide computerized data bases on requested topics. This package of services, called WESTFORNET when it was expanded to include the RM Station and Regions in its territory, was made available from the Rocky Mountain Station library to the Regional Offices and down to the District Ranger level in Regions 1, 2, 3, and 4. The Alerts were also made available to other resource agencies (including BLM and BIA) and some forestry schools. Station scientists also used the service, especially the literature-searching capability. Information Specialist Bob Dana developed a strong reputation for designing productive,

carefully focused literature searches, which then generated demands on the document delivery service. The Alerts alone could generate requests for hundreds of documents monthly.

Because the Regional Offices paid for the bulk of the costs of WESTFORNET/FS INFO, under the "user pay" philosophy, continuation of the entire package of services was dependent on National Forest System support, which generally ended in the late 90's.

HELP Line

Director Hank Montrey instituted the *HELP Line*, a "hot line" telephone service intended to provide quick answers or at least a referral to someone who might be able to provide a quick answer to FS professionals throughout the Station's territory. Kicked off with much fanfare

about another new tool to improve communication between researchers and resource managers, the HELP Line phone rang frequently on Bob Hamre's desk, with support from Rick Fletcher. Use faded over time, and the HELP Line was turned off at Bob's retirement in 1993.

Electronic Publishing

Electronic publishing was just reaching functional acceptance in the mid 90's. Journals were accepting submissions in electronic format, author-formatted symposium papers were being accepted on disks, and some highly specialized journals were being published "on the web."

Nothing, however, seemed poised to replace synergy generated by face-to-face communication in the field, backed up by understandable, useable, printed documentation.

Library staff in the early 1990s, from left: Angie Ruble, Frances Barney, Kathy Munoz, Carin Batt, Bob Dana, Marie Zegar and Gene Kennedy.

A planning meeting of Mexican and U.S. foresters at the Fraser Experimental Forest, around 1994.
Bottom row, left to right: *Cele Aguirre Bravo (RM), Denver Burns (RM), Hugo Manzanilla (INIFAP), Ernesto Samayoa Dominquez (INIFAP), Jerry Sesco (WO), Alberto Gomez Tagle (INIFAP).* ***Middle row:*** *Fernando Patino Valera (INIFAP), Deborah Chavez (INIFAP), Marcia Patton Mallory (RM), Reynaldo Valenzuela (INIFAP), Gonsalo Navelo Gonzales (INIFAP), M. Lacayo Emery (WO), Deborah Shields (RM), Francisco Javier Musalem Lopez (INIFAP).* ***Back row:*** *unidentified, Bill Rietveld (RM), Carlos Gonzales Vicente (INIFAP), Andrea Koonce (WO), Terry Shaw (RM), Ed Green (FPL), Raphael Moreno (INIFAP), Sam Sandberg (PNW).*

Cooperation With Mexico

Although records of coopera- tion between forestry professionals in Mexico and the U.S. go back as far as 1911, a Regional Agreement signed by Acting Director Dixie Smith in 1981 to establish technical and scientific collaboration in forestry between the National Institute of Forestry Research in Mexico and the Rocky Mountain Station and Southwestern Region of the USDA Forest Service provided the mechanism for supporting

truly effective cooperation across a political border artificially dividing continuous ecosystems.

The primary tool to assure a continuing program was a series of roughly biennial symposia, with locations alternating between the two countries. The first, *Management and Utilization of Arid Land Plants,* held in Saltillo, Coahuila, in February 1985, was coordinated primarily by David Patton, RM Station, and Carlos Gonzalez-Vicente, Instituto

Nacional de Investigaciones Forestales y Agropecuarias (INIFAP, within SARH, the Secretaria de Agricultura y Recursos Hidraulicos). The second, *Strategies for Classification and Management of Native Vegetation for Food Production in Arid Zones,* was held in Tucson, AZ, in October 1987. *Integrated Management of Watersheds for Multiple Uses* followed in March 1990 in Morelia, Michoacan, then

Making Sustainability Operational in Santa Fe, NM, in April 1993. The fifth symposium in the series, *Partnerships for Sustainable Forest Ecosystem Management,* in October 1994 in Guadalajara, Jalisco, stressed building research-management partnerships among natural resource managers, scientists, landowners, policymakers, and public interest groups.

A corollary objective of the frequent symposium series was to create opportunities for individual researchers and managers to develop mutually beneficial one-on-one cross-border working relationships.

Gonzalez-Vicente was an imposing presence throughout the period; Avelino Villa-Salas, Hugo Manzanilla, and Leonel Iglesias Gutierrez were also major contributors for Mexico. Tom Schmeckpeper, John Russell, and Doug Shaw were major players from the Southwestern Region. Dixie Smith, Earl Aldon, Len DeBano, Bob Hamre, and several others from RM Station contributed significantly. Bob Partido (SW Region) and George Garcia (RM Station) were invaluable in maintaining smooth informal communications, since most U.S. participants had nowhere near the bilingual capabilities of their Mexican counterparts. Although virtually every Mexican spoke passable English, there were professional translators for the technical sessions. Dan Neary, Debbie Finch, and Carl Edminster were involved in the later symposia.

In addition to the formal biennial series, *Biodiversity and Management of the Madrean Archipelago: the Sky Islands of Southwestern United States and Northwestern Mexico*, in Tucson in September 1994, was also a major cross-border effort.

In 1994, Cele Aguirre-Bravo came to the Station to coordinate cooperative efforts between INIFAP and the Rocky Mountain Station, and had the lead for subsequent symposia. The Rocky Mountain Station has now extended its cooperation and collaboration activities to other countries in the Americas. These activities are coordinated through the Consortium for Advancing the Monitoring of Ecosystem Sustainability in the Americas (CAMESA). CAMESA's program activities are coordinated by the Rocky Mountain Station.

A Sampling of Major Characters at RM Station

Any time you take a sample, there is chance you will miss something important. The alternatives here are to say nothing or mention everyone. Neither of those is appropriate, so at the risk of offending the many worthy of mention, we'll take a sample. A preponderance are retired.

The Leadership Team – When David Herrick retired in November 1980, Dixie Smith was appointed Acting Director. About a year later, Charles Loveless arrived from the Washington Office to take the helm, with Dixie Smith continuing as Deputy Director. Charlie, who had spent many years with the USDI Fish and Wildlife Service, was Director for 8 years, retiring in June 1989. In October, Henry (Hank) Montrey came West from the Forest Products Laboratory to become the eighth Director of the Rocky Mountain Station. Hank moved on to the Washington Office, and Denver Burns traded his Directorate at the Northeast Station to become our ninth Director in October 1992. In November 1993, Chief Robertson also gave Denver the role of Acting Director of the Intermountain Station, another sign of the pending merger of the two Stations.

Indispensable to the Directors were their Secretaries: Barbara Gary, Debbie Allen (*now Hof*), and Martha Pforr.

Dixie Smith put in 11 loyal years as Deputy Director of the RM

Todd Mowrer (in uniform), along with Technicians Manual Martinez, Steve Mata, Jose Negron and other Station employees host high school students at the annual Hispanic Natural Resources Career Camp at the Fraser Experimental Forest.

Station. Harold Paulsen, Sam Krammes, Tom Hoekstra, and Marcia Patton-Mallory successively held the title of Assistant Director for Planning and Applications. Assistant Directors for Research included David Tackle, Vincent Duvall, Clyde Fasick, Richard Krebill, Stephen McDonald, Tom Hoekstra, and Ed Wicker.

Two Rocky Mountain Station "graduates" went on to become Forestry School Deans within the Station's territory: Jay Hughes at Colorado State University, and Dave Garrett at Northern Arizona University.

Scientists – No listing of RM scientists of the era would be complete without citing people

such as Bob Alexander (timber management and Fraser Experimental Forest), Frank Hawksworth (dwarf mistletoes), Pete Martinelli and Ron Tabler (blowing snow), Art Judson (avalanches), Bev Driver (recreation), Earl Aldon, Jerry Horton, and Len DeBano (southwestern watersheds), Clark Martin (southwestern ranges), Ralph Read (shelterbelts), Glenn Peterson (pathology), Jack Dieterich (fire), Dick Tinus (containerized seedlings), George Peterson (economics), Dave Patton (southwestern wildlife), Gil Schubert (southwestern timber), Dick Driscoll (range, remote sensing) and Doug Fox (atmospheric sciences). They were some of the well-known

Project Leader/scientists. All of them relied heavily on the input and support of talented project scientists, many of whom show up on group and research photos throughout this history.

Technicians – Technicians are often the unsung heroes of research. RM Station has been blessed with several great technicians, often the essential glue that held complex projects and project locations together. They provided the practical links between research ideas and actual collection and presentation of data. They were contact points between researchers and cooperators, translators, electronics specialists, jacks-of-all-trades. Outstanding among them were George Garcia at Albuquerque, Steve Mata at Fort Collins, Harvey Hiatt at Bottineau and Flagstaff, Bob

Ted Hovland, Lincoln, pollinates selected Scots pine in one of Ralph Read's provenance plantations for improving Great Plains shelterbelts.

Jairell at Laramie, Ross Watkins at Fort Collins and Manitou Experimental Forest, Bill Kruse at Flagstaff and the Santa Rita Experimental Range, Manuel Martinez at Fraser Experimental Forest, Steve Denison at Rapid City, and John Sprackling at Lincoln. *(Steve Mata remains active in 2004.)*

Ted Hovland at Lincoln presented a unique problem. At a lanky 6' 7" he made even the best young trees look small in Ralph Read's photos documenting shelterbelt provenance studies. The problem was resolved with role reversal: Ted became the photographer and Ralph provided the size perspective.

Professional Support – A key in quality control at RM Station was *(and still is)* Rudy King. As Station Biometrician, he provided guidance on research design, and evaluation and interpretation of data. His insightful evaluations of the most complex manuscripts in every field of research from avalanches to zoology were the envy of the other Stations, and a particular boon to the Station Editor.

Bob Hamre gave decades of solid editorial support for the Station's scientists, generating the Station's serial publications and providing links with a host of technical journals. His techniques for ramrodding symposium proceedings into print quickly made the Station a major host for a variety of major symposia. The

library and Frances Barney were interchangeable names for the place to go for anyone needing help finding old – and new – literature. Frances may have been on a first-name basis with more front-line people on the National Forests in the Regions we serve than any other person at the Station.

Administration – Don Keefer, Jackie Cables, and Harold Coley had the daunting task of heading up what was called Research Support Services. That included Bill North's Operations Group (personnel, fiscal, administrative services), Biometrics (for a time), and the Research Information Group (publications, public affairs, library). Clarence Adair, a computer programmer for many years, found his calling as the gregarious leader of the Station's civil rights program. LeRoy Manley headed up Personnel for many years, while Harold Kehr and Sue Janzen (now Evans) contributed years of leadership in fiscal and administrative services.

At the project locations, people such as Zita Kaulitz (Rapid City), Vera Collins (Laramie), Lucille Neubauer (Bottineau), Josie Gomez and Nancy Muecke (Tempe), Virginia Hittner (Lincoln), Nora Altamirano (Albuquerque), and Marion Durham, Diane Prince, and Judy Kent (Flagstaff and Tempe) worked many years under a variety of titles to provide business, computer, and secretarial support.

A technician takes readings, winter and summer, at the Snowy Range station on the Glacier Lakes Ecosystem Experiments Site, Wyoming, as part of the National Atmospheric Deposition Program.

How Some Station Research Has Been Applied

The RM Station took form in 1930 with an annual appropriation of $75,000: $25,000 each for research on range, watershed, and timber management. Highlights of early research accomplishments were chronicled in Ray Price's 1976 history. What advances have we made since then?

As Director Hank Montrey put it in 1991, "Some ... research success was short-lived because it only solved an immediate, local problem. Some of it was of lasting significance because it helped us understand underlying processes. Some generated unexpected benefits, while some simply

contributed to the knowledge base of specific scientific disciplines. Some of the latter is still in search of utility, but it is this bank of knowledge we frequently draw upon when new problems arise."

Among the many things we learned from the long-running, multifunctional Beaver Creek Watershed south of Flagstaff, for instance, was how difficult it is to model an ecosystem!

Again, Montrey philosophized about what research is all about: "We must obviously move from the functional, single-resource, single-scientist focus on physical and biological sciences aimed at advancing science in a discipline.

We need to move toward inter-disciplinary, multi-resource, integrated teams that include social scientists.... If we are to have much influence over our future, we must develop an over-riding customer ethic in what we do. Instead of looking *inward* to our own interests and disciplines for guidance in structuring our research efforts, we need to do a better job of looking *outward* to the land managers, resource users, policy makers, and various publics we *serve* for that guidance."

Forest Service Chief Jack Ward Thomas also waxed philosophically when responding to

23

questions during a Congressional budget hearing. A Congressman, referring to the Forest Service theme "Caring for the land, serving the people," questioned "Who *are* you serving?" Jack simply replied, "The vast majority of the people we serve *haven't been born yet!"*

Much of our research results in incremental gains in knowledge. We've solved many current problems, but along the way we've also broadened the scope and depth of what we know about the physical and biological processes that affect how ecosystems work. For example, Jack Dieterich's pioneering work on fire history and fire return intervals in southwestern forests in the '70's and '80's was originally applied in prescribed fire. Now it is contributing significantly to our current broader understanding of the essential role of fire in maintaining healthy forest ecosystems. We've banked a lot of information that will ultimately help answer many questions we haven't figured out how to ask yet. That information bank includes a number of plant keys and manuals, floristic inventories of specific geographic areas, and systems to classify biotic communities, habitat types, and ecosystems.

From 1976 to 1997, with the advancement of personal computers, Station research became increasingly quantitative with models, not only the typical timber growth and yield models, but also contributions to fire weather, optimization models

used in land management planning, habitat models for wildlife species, multiresource interaction models, and models for many other natural resources. And we addressed new topics during this period – air quality, nonmarket values, larger spatial scales (national assessments of forest and rangeland resources), riparian ecology – and expanded our scope from timber and range productivity to multiple resource values of ecosystems and cultural implications.

When evaluating research accomplishments, a gnarly question is, "How do we value the significance of a broad range of research findings?" Simply counting publications and consultations isn't enough. Ideally, the value of research shows up when it influences management practices. But not all research finds quick application. A recent approach is the citation index, a measure of the frequency with which a

research publication is cited in the world literature. A 1994 paper in *Forest Science* on reduced photosynthesis rate in old trees, coauthored by Mike Ryan, was still cited about 100 times in 2002! A paper in *Nature* by Dick Sommerfeld and others in 1993 on carbon dioxide flux from soil through a snowpack continues to be cited in environmental and global-change journals worldwide because of its unanticipated implications for global budgets of this greenhouse gas.

The following are a few examples of how Station research findings over the 1976 to 1997 period have been – or may be – widely applied.

Snow Fences

The elaborate system of snow fences along many miles of Interstate 80 west of Laramie, WY, is the direct result of years of

Ron Tabler, Laramie, records data on snow accumulation behind one of the snow fences protecting Interstate 80 west of Laramie, WY (1982). Engineered snow fences can trap large amounts of blowing snow in long drifts higher than the fences (which may be 12 feet tall), greatly reducing plowing costs and highway closures, improving visibility along the highway, and providing water for livestock and wildlife during snowmelt.

research on the physics of trapping blowing snow. What started out as an effort to augment water yields from winter snowpacks on Pole Mountain in the Medicine Bow National Forest for the city of Cheyenne laid the foundation for an unanticipated long-term cooperative program with the Wyoming Highway Department. Drifting snow plagued the highway with closures and accidents. Ron Tabler (Laramie) led studies on transport and evaporation of blowing snow; most effective density, spacing, and height of snow fences; shape, volume, and placement of created snow drifts; and benefits to highway safety and maintenance. The resulting system of snow fences not only drastically reduced snow plowing costs and highway closures, but also improved conditions so much that fence costs could be amortized within as little as 2 years from reduced accident costs alone.

Tabler's research has been published as *Design Guidelines for Control of Blowing And Drifting Snow* by the Strategic Highway Research Program of the National Research Council (see citation in *A Few Significant Publications*), and is being used nationwide in a variety of related snow control and accumulation applications. An unexpected value is that many snow fences are not dismantled after 3 to 5 years, sold as weathered barn wood panels, and new fences are reconstructed.

Richard Reynolds, Fort Collins, and Prof. Tom Gavin, Cornell University (left), band a male northern goshawk on the Kaibab Plateau north of the Grand Canyon in Arizona.

Goshawk Management Recommendations

Present forest conditions – loss of shrubby understory, reduced amount of older forests, increased areas of dense tree regeneration – often reflect the extent of human influence on these forests. These influences may also affect populations of the northern goshawk. In response to litigation in the Southwest, Richard Reynolds (Fort Collins/Flagstaff) and a team appointed by the Regional Forester, Southwest Region, evaluated earlier research by Reynolds and others on goshawk nesting habitat and foraging behavior, and on food and habitats of the suite of important goshawk prey, then synthesized what they learned to develop a set

of "desired forest conditions" and offered management recommendations to move existing forest conditions to the desired conditions for supporting viable goshawk populations. Key objectives of the guidelines are to provide nesting, postfledging, and foraging areas for goshawks, and habitat to support abundant populations of 14 primary goshawk prey. These guidelines have since been validated by 10 years of intensive research on the goshawk on the Kaibab Plateau in northern Arizona.

Thinning trees in the understory, creating small openings around groups of trees in the forest, and prescribed fires should help produce and maintain desired forest conditions. Other critical elements for both goshawks and their prey are large-diameter snags and downed logs, and an all-aged forest composed of highly interspersed groups of similar-aged trees across the goshawk's home range.

Reynolds' *Management Recommendations for the Northern Goshawk in the Southwestern United States* (see citation in *A Few Significant Publications*) are now being used, with appropriate modifications for local forest types, nationwide. Use of the guidelines has also had significant legal implications in environmental lawsuits.

Glenn Peterson's research (Lincoln) on the biology and control of phomopsis blight minimized a major problem in Great Plains nurseries, and allowed them to greatly increase production of eastern red cedar seedlings for shelterbelt plantings.

Tree Diseases on the Great Plains

Diseases of Trees in the Great Plains, a publication produced by Jerry Riffle and Glenn Peterson at the Station's Shelterbelt Laboratory at Lincoln, NE, has been the most frequently re-printed publication in the Station's history. Recognizing the reputations of Riffle and Peterson as leading tree pathology researchers in the area, the Great Plains Agricultural Research Council asked them to coordinate a technical publication

that arborists, land owners, pathologists, pest management specialists, and others desperately needed to diagnose, treat, and prevent tree diseases in shelterbelts in the stressful environment of the Great Plains. The two Station scientists recruited another 29 pathologists, and together they authored over 60 articles on hosts, distribution, symptoms, disease cycle, and control measures for 46 hardwood and 15 conifer diseases.

The publication has been distributed by State Foresters and Extension Specialists throughout the Plains States, and used in graduate school forest pathology courses.

Greenhouses for Containerized Tree Seedlings

Today's extensive greenhouse nursery production of containerized conifer seedlings requires careful control not only of temperature and moisture, but nutrients, light intensity, and photoperiod. Richard Tinus pioneered the science of containerized nurseries, first at Bottineau, ND, then at Flagstaff, AZ.

His research covered use of irrigation water and soil medium to deliver nutrients, levels of light intensity for photosyhsthesis and growth, intermittent light to control photoperiod and prevent dormancy for continuous seedling growth, design of containers and treatment of inner surfaces to direct root growth, and inducing dormancy and cold-hardiness of

Dick Tinus, Flagstaff, evaluates bristlecone pine seedlings grown in containers under sodium arc light from a "beam flicker" in a Colorado State Forest Service nursery.

seedlings before storage and outplanting. Working closely with other Forest Service nursery specialists, Tinus coauthored the six-volume Agriculture Handbook 674, The Container Tree Nursery Manual (citation in *A Few Significant Publications*) used worldwide.

Resource Planning Act Assessments

When Tom Hoekstra came to the Station (Fort Collins) from the WO in 1979 to join the Resource Evaluation Techniques Program, he brought with him the task of preparing the Wildlife and Fish component of the RPA Assessment. The Resources Planning Act of 1975 mandates this national assessment by the Forest Service every 10 years, with an intermediate, fifth-year update. The result is a comprehensive document that addresses the recent historical, current, and probable future status of the nation's forest and rangeland resources. For the 1984 assessment update, scientists in Hoekstra's unit were selected to evaluate three of the six major resource areas. In addition to Hoekstra's wildlife and fish area, Linda Joyce handled range, and John Hof dealt with multi-resource integration. Later, John Mitchell assumed responsibility for the range assessment, Curt Flather took over wildlife and fish, and Linda Joyce was responsible for the climate change special assessment study. Tom Brown led the water assessment. These were monumental tasks.

In addition to broad science responsibilities for the 1989 Assessment and 1994 Update, the RM Station also assumed responsibility for editing, printing, and distributing the entire expanded collection of 11 separate resource documents. Under Editor Bob Winokur's guidance, the Station generated and mailed *tons* of these documents (see reports by Brown, Flather, and Joyce in *A Few Significant Publications*) to Federal, State, and local governmental agencies, interest groups, and concerned individuals across the nation, and indeed throughout the world. The Station has continued its role as the major player in the national RPA Assessment effort. The number of resource-oriented topics has increased, authors have changed, and some publication responsibilities have been shifted to other Stations, but to the WO, RPA still equates with RMRS.

John Lundquist (left), Fort Collins, and a technician examine root rot at the base of a pine subsequently killed by bark beetles. Note the globs of pitch produced by the tree in an unsuccessful attempt to repel the beetles.

Valuing Nonmarket Resources

Through years of pioneering research, members of George Peterson's (Fort Collins) Research Work Unit on Identification and Valuation of Wildland Resource Benefits have developed ways to identify and evaluate the monetary and non-monetary benefits of wildland management. In addition to numerous publications in scientific and applied journals and other forums, they have produced several important books, including *Public Amenity Resource Valuation: Integrating Economics with Other Disciplines; Valuing Wildlife Resources in Alaska; Instream Flow Protection;* and *Nature and the Human Spirit: Toward an Expanded Land Management Ethic* (see citations in *A Few*

Significant Publications). The unit's research findings have been widely used, both in this country and around the world, in such diverse applications as the Resource Planning Act's Assessment and Program, the Exxon-Valdez tanker spill damage assessment in Alaska, forest health policy, water resource management and valuation, sensitive species conservation, fire management policy, and the United Nations Environmental Program's Global Biodiversity Assessment. Because the unit's scientists have been active in many national and international activities, including leadership in the International Union of Forest Research Organizations, Fulbright exchanges, and invited lectures and consultations in many foreign countries, they have received numerous Forest Service Superior and Distinguished Scientist awards.

Ecosystem Management

General Technical Report RM-246, *An Ecological Basis for Ecosystem Management,* published in 1994 helped establish ecosystem management as a basis for land stewardship. A team of scientists and managers from a number of Federal and State agencies prepared this publication, with Station Scientist Merrill Kaufmann (Fort Collins) as senior author (see citation in *A Few Significant Publications*). The team illustrated that social and economic issues play a large role in attaining ecological sustainability, while ecological capability of land is relatively fixed. Achieving ecological sustainability may thus require adjustments in social and economic perspectives. The publication provides guidelines for examining ecosystems to determine their current condition, and to identify what might be needed to maintain or restore ecological sustainability. These guidelines used conservation biology principles and historical and current conditions at multiple spatial and temporal scales as the basis for ecological assessment.

This publication also helped place ecological issues on the same level as social and economic issues in the decisionmaking process. Previously, many natural resource management decisions had been made with limited emphasis on long-term ecological consequences of human activities. The team's findings helped clarify how and where in the planning process ecological issues could be addressed, and outlined how monitoring and evaluation could provide feedback to improve

Joe Ganey checks the fit of a radio transmitter prior to releasing a Mexican spotted owl in a study of owl habitat needs.

decisions in the ongoing planning and implementation process collectively known as adaptive management. The approaches outlined have been used widely in the development and implementation of natural resource plans, and have had a significant influence on land stewardship. The current approach of using historical ecology in 21st century decision-making stems directly from the importance of reference condition information in ecosystem assessments noted in the GTR.

A Different Perspective on Forest Diseases

Traditionally, forest disease research has focused primarily on stand-scale timber production systems, where diseases were viewed as harmful because they killed trees and reduced timber productivity. With a better

understanding of forest ecology, however, perspectives on diseases have expanded to the point where they are viewed as natural components of landscapes that may have neutral, detrimental, or beneficial impacts on ecological processes and landscape patterns that perhaps should be preserved or even mimicked. Landscape pathology was introduced by station pathologists as an extension of our traditional view of forest pathology.

Spatial analyses, spatial modeling, and other landscape-scale methods of assessing and quantifying disease impacts based on spatial patterns have been developed by station pathologists to examine the effects of diseases on wildfire fuels, wildlife diversity, and other timber and nontimber resources. An assessment and monitoring method called profiling was developed to simplify and quantify the complex impacts symptomatic of diseased landscapes. Station pathologists have also developed methods for measuring and quantifying similarity of canopy gaps caused by diseases and other types of disturbance (insects, wind, fire, etc) so the their impacts can be mimicked in gap-based silviculture (see Lundquist and Beatty, in *A Few Significant Publications*).

Mexican Spotted Owl Recovery Plan

Listing of the Mexican spotted owl as a Threatened Species in 1993 resulted in severe restrictions on forest management in the Southwest. Bill Block (Flagstaff) led a recovery team, including Joe Ganey, Wil Moir, and Pat Ward, to develop a strategy for recovering the owl. They synthesized available information about the owl and its habitat, most of which existed as a direct result of their own studies, and identified the types of habitats and resources key to recovering the owl. They then crafted a recovery strategy that afforded protection to the owl while simultaneously allowing management for other resource values in most of the landscape. This recovery plan (see the USDI report in *A Few Significant Publications*) was formally adopted by the Southwestern Region of the Forest Service through an amendment to the land management plans for each of its National Forests. It is also being used in the Intermountain and Rocky Mountain Regions, the National Park Service, Bureau of Land Management, Department of Defense, and various Indian Tribes throughout the Southwestern United States.

The recovery plan also defined scientifically credible monitoring schemes for owl populations and habitat, and experiments to determine cause-and-effect relationships between forest treatments and trends in key owl habitat and prey. Station scientists continue to serve on the recovery team.

In addition, Bill Block and Debbie Finch (Albuquerque) led an effort to summarize knowledge on songbirds inhabiting ponderosa pine forests in the Southwest. This effort was mandated by a court-ordered settlement agreement in a lawsuit (Silver vs. Thomas, 1996)

pertaining to the owl. Block and Finch assembled a station team, which included Joe Ganey, Brian Geils, Wil Moir, and Carol Raish, to synthesize information on songbird ecology in southwestern ponderosa pine (see Block and Finch citation in *A Few Significant Publications*). This document is now the key reference on ecology of numerous bird species in this vegetation type and geographic area, and resulted in the lifting of an injunction on most forest management activities in the Southwestern Region.

Mine Spoil Reclamation

Basic studies of native plants with potential for revegetating degraded watersheds and ranges in the Southwest were a staple at the Station's Forestry Sciences Lab at Albuquerque. Laboratory studies established initial moisture and temperature requirements for germination of such hardy species as alkali sacaton and four-wing saltbush (a salt-tolerant grass and shrub, respectively). Studies progressed through greenhouse trials to small- and large-scale field plots to factor in seasonal and soil effects. Earl Aldon and Wayne Springfield then took this knowledge to the Surface Environment and Mining (SEAM) program, and applied it to mine spoils exposed after coal was strip-mined in northwestern New Mexico. Their findings were applied to meet revegetation requirements not only on coal mine spoils, but also after uranium and copper mining.

At the Forestry Sciences Laboratory in Rapid City, Ardell Bjugstad, Dan Uresk, and others did similar work with forbs, shrubs, and small trees for revegetating mine spoils in the SEAM program. Bentonite and gold mine spoils were major concerns, in addition to coal and uranium.

The Colorado Avalanche Warning Program

Early in his Forest Service career, Art Judson (Fort Collins) was a Snow Ranger on the Arapaho National Forest and avalanche forecaster on Berthod Pass, northwest of Denver. He joined Pete Martinelli's "Blowing Snow" project at the RM Station in 1962, where he refined his avalanche modeling and prediction techniques through research on the physics of blowing snow and avalanche release, and upgrading and expanding instrumentation in critical high-elevation snow accumulation areas (see his research model, in *A Few Significant Publications*).

The formal Avalanche Warning Program which includes media bulletins, telephone hotline, and awareness training became operational in the 1970s. It continued to evolve, with contributions from Martinelli, R.A. Schmidt, and Colorado State University's Owen Rhea. Knox Williams joined the project in 1970, and took over the warning program by the end of the decade. Knox led the program through a turbulent funding period in the early

Dan Uresk, Rapid City, often relied on Joker to locate collared deer during habitat research with Kieth Severson on the Badlands of South Dakota.

1980s to its current stable operating base, independent of the Forest Service. Its warnings continue to save lives among skiers and other back-country winter recreationists, motorists, snowplow operators, and mountain residents. The program has been duplicated in most other Western States.

Another product of Martinelli's Blowing Snow project was the *Avalanche Handbook*, Agriculture Handbook 489, co-authored by Ron Perla (see *A Few Significant Publications*). First published in 1976, it quickly became a Government Printing Office best-seller among those who worked, played, traveled, or did research in the mountains in winter, worldwide. It was reprinted three times within five years, and translated into several languages.

Maintaining Wildlife on the Great Plains

As human-related pressures increase on grasslands of the northern Great Plains, resource managers need better tools to monitor how plants, and the wildlife species that depend on them, may be responding to impacts on the natural environment. To fill the need, Research Biologist Dan Uresk at the Rapid City Forestry Sciences Laboratory, working with Station Biometrician Rudy King, used elaborate statistical techniques to develop easily-applied methods managers can use to evaluate range conditions (see Uresk 1990, in *A Few Significant Publications*). His research identified key plant variables managers can measure to

discriminate among ecological stages, then establish resource value ratings that can be used to guide decisions on resource uses, including livestock grazing, and predict their impacts on wildlife. His vegetation-based methods are not only easy and accurate, but predict responses of wildlife even rare species faster than methods that require monitoring the animals themselves. Uresk's successful efforts to get this research applied quickly over a variety of habitats earned him the prestigious New Perspectives Award from Forest Service Chief Dale Roberston in 1992.

Dwarf Mistletoe Impacts

Frank Hawksworth's decades of research on the biology and classification of the world's dwarf mistletoes laid the groundwork for subsequent models to predict the impact of these host-specific plants on growth of various forest trees. Hawksworth (Fort Collins) and Carl Edminster combined to write several computer models (RMYIELD, etc) so that managers could estimate future growth and yields of infected forests. *Dwarf Mistletoes: Biology, Pathology, and Systematics*, an Agriculture Handbook by Hawksworth and Wiens, will likely remain a classic text for students, researchers, and managers for decades.

Increased Water Yield Through Forest Management

Chuck Troendle's (Fort Collins) research in high-elevation forests at the Fraser Experimental Forest in Colorado in the late 70's and early 80's clearly documented that the portion of increased water yield due to increased snow accumulation after any pattern of partial harvest was primarily due to reduced evaporation from snow intercepted on foliage. This finding reversed an earlier interpretation that this increased water yield from snow was almost entirely due to altered aerodynamics and redistribution of intercepted snow into clear-cut openings.

To show that results from such relatively small-scale research could be applied at an operational scale, the Station cooperated with the Rocky Mountain Region in the Coon Creek Water Yield Demonstration Project on the Medicine Bow National Forest in southern Wyoming. After the 4,000-acre Coon Creek and a companion control watershed were carefully calibrated for 7 years, Coon Creek was partially harvested according to Troendle's research-based prescription. The accurately predicted water yields documented that a major forest management project could be implemented with minimal detrimental effect on other resources.

Minimizing Mortality Caused by Bark Beetles

After focusing on the spruce beetle in the 1970s, culminating in his *Spruce Beetle in the Rockies* coauthored with R. H. Frye, John Schmid (Fort Collins, Flagstaff) turned his attention largely to the mountain pine beetle. After working on various aspects of the mountain pine beetle, particularly relating to silvicultural treatments to manage for beetle outbreaks and quantifying beetle-caused mortality in ponderosa and lodgepole pines in Colorado and the Black Hills of South Dakota, Schmid developed a hazard rating system to help land managers rate stand susceptibility to beetles. Since retiring in 1991, Schmid has continued his long-term entomology research as a volunteer.

Measuring the Benefits of Outdoor Recreation

Bev Driver came from the University of Michigan faculty to direct the new Outdoor Recreation Research Work Unit established at the Station in 1973. His focus was to consider all benefits of outdoor recreation: social, economic, and environmental, as well as psychological. With Perry Brown of Colorado State University, he developed the Recreation Opportunity Spectrum (ROS) system for inventorying and managing outdoor recreation resources, a system needed to meet requirements mandated by Congress in the 1976 National Forest Management Act for the

USFS and similar Federal Land Management and Policy Act for the Bureau of Land Management (see Driver et al. 1987, in *A Few Significant Publications*). That system is now used throughout the US, Canada, and many other countries. A related effort resulted in the Wilderness Opportunity Zoning management system, widely used by the USFS and BLM, and which led, in part, to development of the Limits of Acceptable Change concept for managing negative impacts of recreation.

Driver's efforts in developing and editing the book *Benefits of Leisure* (see Driver et al. 1991) significantly advanced our knowledge about the socially important benefits of leisure. That text led to the development of a new approach to evaluating the benefits of leisure called the Beneficial Outcomes Approach to Leisure (BOAL), now being widely taught here and abroad and used to guide allocation decisions by park and recreation policy makers and managers.

Bev Driver's (Fort Collins) recreation research helped identify conflicting motivations and values of recreationists, such as these backpackers, and how those conflicts could be avoided or reduced.

Ecosystem Management in the Southwestern Borderlands

The Southwestern Borderlands project was established in 1994 with Carl Edminster (Flagstaff) as Project Leader. Focused on southeastern Arizona and southwestern New Mexico near the border with Mexico, it is intended to "Contribute to the scientific basis for developing and implementing a comprehensive ecosystem management plan to restore natural processes, improve the productivity and biological diversity of grasslands and woodlands, and sustain an open landscape with a viable rural economy and social structure in the region." Numerous partners, including the Malpai Borderlands Group, USDA Natural Resources Conservation Service, Animas Foundation, Coronado National Forest, The Nature Conservancy, universities, and local ranchers, are cooperating to apply knowledge gained from earlier range, wildlife, fire, and watershed research to management of both private and public lands. These practical applications also provide opportunities for further research on management-scale implementation of research results. Reintroduction of fire as an ecological restoration tool is one of the more significant efforts.

Maintaining Streamflow in the West's Rivers

Maintaining adequate instream flow is a critical concern, especially in the West where water tends to be scarce. The National Forests play a key role in maintaining instream flow because they are the source of much of the West's water. In *Instream Flow Protection: Seeking a Balance in Western Water Use* (see citation in *A Few Significant Publications*), Tom Brown (Fort Collins) and coauthor David Gillilan provided a comprehensive overview of Western water use and the issues that surround it. The authors explained instream flow and its historical, political, and legal context; described instream flow laws and policies; and presented methods of protecting instream flow. They provided numerous examples to illustrate their discussions, with case studies of major river systems including the Bitterroot, Clark's Fork, Colorado, Columbia, Platte, Snake, Wind, and others. This book helped numerous groups policymakers, land and water managers at local, State, and Federal levels, attorneys, students and researchers of water issues, and others concerned with instream flow protection gain a richer understanding of Western water management in general and of instream flow protection in particular.

In other publications (for example, see the paper on the Colorado River Basin in *A Few Significant Publications*) Brown determined the value of water yield increases due to forest management by simulating the routing, storage, and delivery of water yield increases throughout the watershed. His results showed that - because of the timing of the increases in the management of reservoirs - much of the increases evaporate or flow on to the sea, and thus their value tends to be less than expected.

Rocky Mountain Forest and Range Experimen

240 West Prospect Road
Fort Collins, Colorado 80526
(303) 498-1100, FTS-8-303-498-1100

Thomas Hoekstra
Assistant Station
Director, Research

Brian M. Kent
Resource Assessment
Ecology and Management
RWU-4802

Leonard F. Ruggiero
Wildlife Habitat
Relationships
RWU-4251

Leonard F. DeBano
Southwestern Watersheds
RWU-4302

Robert C. Musselman
(Acting) Effects of
Atmospheric Changes
RWU-4452

Charles B. Edminster
Multiresource
Management
RWU-4151

Douglas G. Fox
Program Manager
Interior West Global
Change RD&A Program
RWU-4453

George Peterson
(Acting) Cultural
Resources Research, Econ
RWU-4853

Charles G. Shaw III
Pest Impact Assessment
RWU-4851

Russ T. Schroeder
Multiresource Inventory
Techniques
RWU-4802

Earl F. Aldon
Southwestern Grassland
Watersheds
RWU-4251

John G. Hof
Economics and
Optimization for Forestry
RWU-4803

Rudy M. King
Biostatistics and Resource
Data Systems

Russell W. Chase
Grassland and Wildlife
Habitat
RWU-4252

Charles A. Troendle
Watershed and Riparian
Research
RWU-4301

Richard M. Town
Stress Physiology of
Western Conifers
RWU-4152

George L. Peterson
Valuation of Wildland
Resource Benefits
RWU-4851

William Block (Acting)
Management Effects on
Fish, Wildlife and Water
RWU-4251

34

Denver Burns
Station Director

Marcia Patton-
Mallory
Assistant Station
Director, Planning
and Applications

Harold G. Goley
Assistant Station
Director,
Administration

R. Wayne White
Project Manager
Special Project

Larry Behrens
Western Systems
Technology Center

William L. Boyd, Jr.
Group Leader Operations

Clarence O. Huff
Group Leader
Administrative Systems
Support and Equipment
Technology

Larry W. Sandoval
Innovation Coordinator

Mike J. Roesvel
Program Manager
Center for Semiarid
Agroforestry

Robert P. Winokur
Information Management
Officer

Robert H. Hamre
Group Leader Research
Information

Michele Schoeneberger
Great Plains
Tree Improvement
RWU-4251

Joseph D. Mitchell
Native American
Educational Liaison

A Timeline of Significant and/or Interesting Events
at the Rocky Mountain Station

This timeline is intended not only to document many of the important events at the Station over the period 1976 to 1997, but also to provide some insights into the character and daily life of the people who made up the Rocky Mountain Forest and Range Experiment Station's extended family during that period. Most of the dates have been gleaned from Rick Fletcher's Rocky Mountain Update and Director's Notes newsletters.

Dick Sommerfeld, Fort Collins, contemplates the entrance to a buried research structure on the Glacier Lakes Ecosystem Experiments Site in southern Wyoming.

January '76   Evaluation of Watershed Programs in the Salt-Verde River Basin in Tucson is combined with Beaver Creek National Multiple Use Evaluation Project in Flagstaff.

The RWU Economics of Recreation Related Developments in the Rocky Mountain West RWU in Fort Collins is terminated; Gordon Lewis becomes Program Manager of the Eisenhower Consortium for Western Environmental Forestry Research in Fort Collins.

The SEAM (Surface Environment and Mining) program reports adopting Plant Physiologist Dick Tinus' (Flagstaff) containerized seedling approach for revegetating mine spoils.

Clerical workers throughout the Station were united under the banner of the Clerical Staff Organization, with Clerk Helen Waag (Fort Collins) as first chairperson.

March '76   National Renewable Resource Supply and Evaluation Techniques becomes an R&D program: Resources Evaluation Techniques. Dick Driscoll (Fort Collins) is Program Manager.

In an RWU realignment, three Fort Collins projects   Forest and Mountain Meteorology, Developing More Productive Markets for Forest Resources of the Rocky Mountains and Adjacent High Plains, and Development and Application of a National Fuel Inventory and Appraisal System   now report to Vincent Duvall, AD for Continuing Research, Tempe, AZ.

April '76   Stan Hirsch is named Project Leader for the new National Fuel Inventory and Appraisal System RWU (Fort Collins).

May '76   Director and staff spend 3 days focusing on how to develop Station research programs to meet the goals of the Resources Planning Act.

Scientists R.A. Schmidt (Fort Collins) and Ron Tabler (Laramie) receive the USDA Superior Service Award in Washington for adapting their research results ". . .into the operational procedures needed to monitor and control blowing snow under severe winter conditions along the Interstate Highway through Wyoming."

June '76   At Laramie, two projects are combined to form RM-1712, Land Use Impacts on Big Game and Ecological Relationships of Mining, with Lorin Ward as Project Leader.

Josie Gomez (Tempe) is the new Spanish-Speaking Program Coordinator for the Station.

July '76   The Station completes its three series "status of knowledge" papers, on Timber, Watershed, and Range Management Research.

The Multiresource Management for Southwest Semidesert Rangelands RWU (RM-1706) is combined with the Habitat Criteria Development for Southwestern Wildlife RWU (RM-1710) at Tempe, with Dave Patton as Project Leader.

Six researchers from the Pacific Southwest Station come to Dick Driscoll's Resource Evaluation Techniques Program (R&D RM-4151): Bob Aldrich, Bob Dana, Wally Greentree, Norm Merritt, Dick Myhre, and Ed Roberts.

Some 115 people attend the Station picnic/barbeque (Dick Sommerfeld and Pat Currie, Fort Collins, volunteer as chefs) at Demmel Lake near Waverly, CO.

September '76   Dave Tackle comes from the WO to be Assistant Director for Continuing Research at Fort Collins.

Station scientists Tom Mills, Jim LaBau, Pat Currie, and Dave Patton take on significant assignments for the 1979 RPA Assessment.

November '76   Josie Gomez, Spanish-Speaking Program (Albuquerque), Barbara Gary, Federal Women's Program (Fort Collins), and Deputy Director Dixie Smith are in the WO for a Service-wide Civil Rights Program gathering.

December '76   Project Leader Pete Martinelli's (Fort Collins) Avalanche Handbook is published as Agriculture Handbook 489.

Funding is approved for an extension of the Laramie lab.

January '77   Len DeBano is the new Project Leader for Multiresource Response Evaluation Southwest Watersheds (RM-1606) in Tempe.

February '77   The Director's Office staff, Project Leaders, and Program Managers meet in Tempe to discuss research planning and management.

March '77   Directors of the Intermountain (Roger Bay) and Rocky Mountain (Dave Herrick) Stations meet in Denver to discuss coordination of research efforts.

April '77   The newly funded wildlife unit at Texas Tech, Lubbock, has been officially titled the Great Plains Wildlife Research Laboratory. The Forest Hydrology Lab at Tempe has been retitled Forestry Sciences Laboratory.

Scientist Dick Sommerfeld (Fort Collins) takes project clerks, secretaries, and other personnel on a rugged field trip to Berthoud Pass and Mines Peak to observe equipment for monitoring blowing snow and predicting avalanches.

June '77   Dick Krebill comes to Tempe as Assistant Director for Research, replacing Vinse Duvall.

*Staff at the Forestry Sciences Lab in Lincoln in the mid-1970s. **From left:** Glenn Peterson, Jerry Riffle, Mike Kuhl, Ted Hovland, Virginia Pierson, John Sprackling, David VanHaverbeke, Ralph Read, and James Walla.*

July '77   J. Sam Krammes is the new Assistant Director for Planning and Application, replacing Bud Paulsen, who retired.

Scientist Frank Ronco is reassigned to Flagstaff to head the Culture of Southwest Conifers and Aspen unit.

September '77   Jay Hughes, former Economist at the Station in Fort Collins, returns to town as Dean of the College of Forestry and Natural Resources at CSU.

Dick Driscoll's Resources Evaluation Techniques Program relocates to the Craddock Building in Fort Collins.

Using Lorin Ward's (Laramie) research, the Wyoming Highway Department constructs nearly 7 miles of 8-foot-high fence to channel deer under Interstate 80 in southern Wyoming.

November '77 Scientist Bev Driver (Fort Collins) reports that this year's contributions to the Combined Federal Campaign by Fort Collins employees was the highest in recent years.

Management specialists at CSU are evaluating several RM Station Work Units to assess the relative effectiveness of multifunctional research work units, identify organizational and individual problems, and develop alternative approaches for improving their effectiveness. A report is due "around the end of the year."

December '77 The November 6 to 10 Project Leaders' Meeting refines overall Station research plans. Working groups came up with priorities, and developed a 3-point Mission Statement:

- Package research results in forms useful to practitioners, and encourage the application of new knowledge and technology for improving resource management to meet the goals of society.
- Obtain a better understanding of the interactions among fundamental processes in forest and range environments so that the effects of management practices on all resources can be predicted.
- Determine how interacting processes affect the costs, results, and benefits to be obtained from alternative management programs.

Fraser Experimental Forest is officially designated a Biosphere Reserve by the Man and Biosphere program.

Fool Creek Watershed, Fraser Experimental Forest.

March '78 WESTFORNET (Western Forest Research Information Network) comes to the RM Station territory. It will include standard library service, plus literature searching and document delivery to National Forests in Regions 2 and 3. Librarian Frances Barney (Fort Collins) will be coordinator.

A contract is awarded for construction of a new Albuquerque lab; Station personnel should move from downtown to the new facility near the airport by the end of the year.

April '78 Station Director Dave Herrick appoints Jack Dieterich, Ron Hibbert, Dave Patton, Frank Ronco, Bev Driver, and Bob Stevens to a newly formed Committee of Scientists. The committee will advise the Directorate on scientific issues, monitor the scientific climate at the Station, recommend changes, and mentor new scientists.

June '78 Scientists Stan Hirsch, Pete Roussopoulos, and Jack Dieterich are working with three Forests in Region 2 to implement and evaluate a new national fire management planning process.

The quarterly Region 2/RM Station Joint Staff Meeting is held in Denver to improve coordination between the two.

Fred Stormer arrives in Lubbock from Michigan Technological University to head the new wildlife habitat research project there.

August '78 Beaver Creek Watershed, south of Flagstaff, is named a Biosphere Reserve by the Man and the Biosphere Program.

Cavity-Nesting Birds of North American Forests, a USDA Agriculture Handbook by Project Leader Dave Patton (Tempe) and others, brings kudos to Chief McGuire.

October '78 The Multiresource Management for Subalpine Forests and the Multiple Use Research in the Montane and Foothills Zones units in Fort Collins are to be combined, with Bob Alexander as Project Leader.

Assistant Director Dick Krebilll and Scientist Ron Hibbert (Fort Collins) brief a delegation of scientists from the People's Republic of China on Forest Service research.

November '78 Station Director Dave Herrick is appointed Federal Co-Chairman of the Western Regional Planning Committee of the Regional and National Agricultural Research Planning System.

December '78 *Protect Your Pines from Bark Beetles*, by scientists Bob Stevens and Bill McCambridge (Fort Collins), is published in cooperation with the Colorado State Forest Service. (*It is reprinted for many years.*)

Burchard Heede, Hydrologist at Tempe, spends a week helping the Manti-LaSalle National Forest plan how to deal with stream dynamics after a massive landslide blocks Manti Creek.

January '79 Station Director Dave Herrick meets with 11 retirees, mostly Project Leaders and Assistant Directors, to bring them up-to-date on what is happening at the Station.

A Stationwide survey shows practically all employees favor continuation of "flexitime."

Scientist Ron Tabler's (Laramie) paper *Visibility in Blowing Snow and Applications in Traffic Operations* receives the National Research Councils's Mickle Award for best paper in the area of operation and maintenance of transportation facilities.

Debbie Finch's (Albuquerque) research showed that the southwestern willow flycatcher has greater nest success and lower brood parasitism by brown-headed cowbirds when it uses boxelder trees in riparian areas in the Southwest.

February '79 Secretary Mona Wolf (Fort Collins) is the new chairperson of the Clerical Staff Organization.

April '79 Forest Service Chief John McGuire talks at a Station Family Meeting about possible reorganization, and how a proposed Department of Natural Resources would affect the Forest Service.

May '79 An Easter photo of the Bottineau Lab shows the building nearly buried in snow.

Merrill Kaufmann has 100-foot cables stretched throughout the first-floor hallways as he constructs unique gas exchange chambers for measuring transpiration rates on different tree species at Fraser.

Debbie Finch, a Coop. Ed. Student with the Habitat Criteria Development Project, Tempe, is spending the summer along the Colorado River in western Arizona studying wildlife in riparian habitat. *[Debbie is now a Project Leader]*

August '79   The Mitigation Symposium: A National Workshop on Mitigating Losses of Fish and Wildlife Habitat, attracts over 600 people to CSU. The Station is a cosponsor, and is publishing the proceedings.

The Resources Evaluation Techniques R&D Program is reorganized into four Research Work Units and three Support Groups: National Land Classification System, Dan Merkel, Project Leader; National Resource Analysis Techniques, Tom Hoekstra, Project Leader; National Resource Inventory Techniques, Gyde Lund, Project Leader; and Remote Sensing for Renewable Natural Resources and Land Management Evaluation, Bob Aldrich, Project Leader. Hans Schreuder is Group Leader for Statistical Support, Glen Brink for Data Support and Computer Systems, and Debbie Allen for Clerical Support.

September '79   Project Leader Pete Martinelli and scientist Dick Sommerfeld (Fort Collins) are major organizers of the Snow in Motion symposium at CSU, attended by 200 scientists representing 14 countries. Art Judson, Knox Williams, Ron Tabler, R.A. Schmidt, and Doug Fox also present papers.

October '79   Dave Tackle retires as Assistant Director for Research at Fort Collins after 38 years of Federal service.

Clyde Fasick comes to the Station from the WO, taking Dave Tackle's place as Assistant Director for Research.

December '79   The *Fort Collins Coloradoan* newspaper features the Station's Avalanche Warning Center, and its new 24-hour telephone hotline.

January '80   Dave Garrett is the new Project Leader for Multiresource Management Evaluation and Improvement, "the Beaver Creek Project," at Flagstaff, replacing Ross Carder.

February '80   The Station's Science Seminar Series begins, with guest speaker Hans Gubler from the Swiss Federal Institute for Snow and Avalanche Research. The biweekly series is intended to provide a forum for visiting scientists, give new Station scientists a chance to speak before a technical audience, and have older scientists bring us up-to-date on their work.

March '80   Barbara Gary is reassigned from Director's Secretary to Equal Opportunity Specialist. Debbie Allen is the new Director's Secretary.

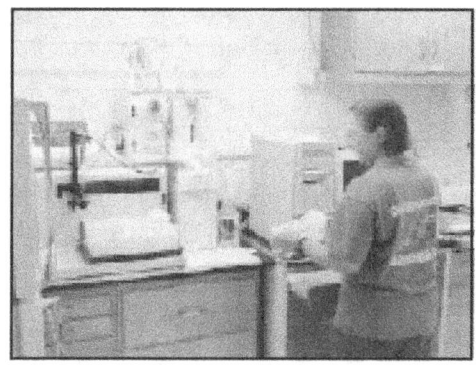

Louise O'Deen analyzes a water sample from Fraser at the Fort Collins Water Laboratory.

May '80   RM Station hosts a conference on "Research on Multiple Use of Forest Resources" at Flagstaff, with 90 scientists from 21 countries attending. The International Union for Forestry Research Organizations and UNESCO's Man and the Biosphere program are cosponsors.

July '80   A new Snow and Avalanche Center at the Station is approved. It is to be a joint effort involving the Station, several Western Forest Service Regions, WO, and Colorado State University.

Scientist Duane Knipe, Tempe, is tending 240 angora goats near Payson, AZ, in a study on bioconversion of chaparral.

October '80 Scientist Dick Sommerfeld (Fort Collins) leaves for a year of work at the Swiss Federal Institute for Snow and Avalanche Research.

RM Station and the Laboratory of Tree-Ring Research sponsor the Fire History Workshop in Tucson.

November '80 Dave Herrick retires as Station Director after 33 years of Federal service; Deputy Director Dixie Smith is Acting Director.

December '80 Arid Land Resource Inventories workshop in LaPaz, Mexico, sets stage for a series of workshops between Mexico, RM Station and Region 3.

Linda Joyce is the new Range Scientist with the National Resource Analysis Techniques unit in Fort Collins.

February '81 Debbie Finch arrives at Laramie as Research Wildlife Biologist with the Land Use Impacts on Big Game unit. *(Both Linda and Debbie later become RM Project Leaders.)*

June '81 Charlie Loveless is named RM Station's seventh Director. He comes from the WO where he was Director of Forest Environment Research.

July '81 The Station's new interactive display, designed by Public Affairs Officer Anne Harrison, is unveiled at the National Audubon Society's biennial convention in Estes Park.

Don Keefer, Assistant Director for Research Support Services, and Gordon Lewis, Program Manager for the Eisenhower Consortium, leave Fort Collins   Don to the Geometronics Service Center in Utah, Gordon to the Southeast Station in Asheville, NC.

The new electronic security system installed at the Headquarters building in Fort Collins replaces keys with a plastic card.

August '81 Scientist Jerry Riffle, Lincoln, spends four weeks in Japan in the Scientist Exchange Program.

October '81 Jackie Cables is appointed Assistant Director for Research Support Services.

At the Project Leaders' Meeting in Fort Collins, Acting Station Director Dixie Smith gives an update on program changes:
- The two projects at Lincoln are combined into a single new one, with Glenn Peterson Project Leader.
- The insect unit at Fort Collins is closed, with personnel reassigned to Bob Alexander's unit.,
- The Resource Evaluation Techniques Program is terminated, and a new R&D Program with two Projects established: Resource Inventory Techniques (Gyde Lund, Project Leader) and Resource Classification (Dan Merkle, Project Leader).
- A new Resource Planning Techniques project will have Tom Hoekstra as Project Leader.
- The Forest Recreation and the Markets and Uses of Forest Resources units are terminated in favor of a new unit, Valuation of Forest Products and Services, with Hal Worth as Acting Project Leader.

The frustrating OMB-imposed moratorium on printing of publications (including our Station's series) will likely be lifted soon, with approval of a USDA publications control plan.

January '82 Station Director Loveless says the uncertain 1982 budget situation is "unsettling for all of us" but "what ever happens, we will do our best to protect people and jobs."

Project Leader Hal Worth (Fort Collins) brings top scientists from around the country to Fort Collins to discuss the issue of assigning values to wildland resource values. George Peterson, Northwestern University, coordinates the presentations. *(In August, George joins the Station to head the new Valuation of Wildland Resource Benefits project, Fort Collins).*

Technicians measure sublimation (evaporation) of intercepted snow on part of water yield studies at the Fraser Experimental Forest.

February '82 Research Forester Chuck Boldt retires at Rapid City after 30 years of Federal service.

Director Loveless kicks off the idea of a "Hobby Corner," where employees can display unique hobbies.

April '82 – WO proposes that, due to proposed budget cuts in FY 83, 30 to 35 Research Work Units will be terminated and nine field locations closed, Servicewide.

Richard Lindeborg, Technical Publications Editor, Fort Collins, is selected as the first "Employee of the Month" for his work with mentally and physically handicapped people in a swimming program.

Some 2,000 hazardous nitrate-based negatives retrieved from around the Station make a spectacular blaze when ignited and destroyed by the Fort Collins Police Department.

Project Leader Pete Martinelli (Fort Collins) is interviewed on the Good Morning America TV show concerning high avalanche incidence in the West.

Computer Specialist Clarence Adair (Fort Collins) coordinates a potluck luncheon as part of Black History Month.

May '82 Project Leader Dave Patton (Tempe) receives one of ten National Conservation Awards, presented in Washington, DC, by Gulf Oil.

June '82 Secretary Fay Pope (Fort Collins) makes Station-sponsored first-aid training pay off by successfully using the Heimlich Maneuver on a choking restaurant patron.

July '82 Ed Wicker comes to the Station as Assistant Director for Research, replacing Dick Krebill, who transfers to the Intermountain Station. Ed will be in Fort Collins, however, rather than Tempe.

The professional employees of the Station vote 31 to 18 to have the National Federation of Federal Employees be their exclusive bargaining agent.

The Station loses three outstanding, long-time Business Management Assistants to retirement: Zita Kaulitz, Rapid City; Vera Collins, Laramie; Lucille Neubauer, Bottineau.

August '82 The 4,000-acre Coon Creek Watershed on the Medicine Bow National Forest in Wyoming is selected as the site for a demonstration project applying research results gained at the Fraser Experimental Forest. Scientist Chuck Troendle will provide Station input.

Smokey Bear shows up, along with some 70 of the Station family, at the Annual Summer Picnic at Mountain Park Campground in Poudre Canyon west of Fort Collins.

Judy Hager, Lead Clerk in the Word Processing Center, is providing training in how to use the new mag card typewriter.

November '82 The Forest Service's National Herbarium, maintained at RM Station headquarters for years, is loaned indefinitely to the University of Wyoming to become part of the Rocky Mountain Herbarium, one of the largest in the Nation.

Scientist R. A. Schmidt (Laramie) will spend the winter in Davos, Switzerland, as part of the Cooperative Scientist Exchange Program.

January '83 Director Charlie Loveless shares his skills and experience in fly tying in a unique Hobby Corner display.

February '83 The Bottineau Lab is officially transferred to North Dakota State University.

From 1967 to 2000, Station headquarters was located at 240 W. Prospect Road in Fort Collins.

March '83 Arapaho-Roosevelt National Forest co-locates with RM Station at Station headquarters. Projected annual savings from shared administrative services: $292,000.

The Station's Lubbock laboratory at Texas Tech closes.

April '83 The Station's first "Outstanding Publication Awards" are announced. First recipients: Ron Tabler for 1980, Merrill Kaufmann 1981, and R. A. Schmidt 1982.

Responding to Project Leaders' concerns at a Project Leaders' Meeting in Fort Collins, Director Loveless proposes development of a Station Direction Statement emphasizing:.
- A shift toward basic, problem-oriented research.
- Increased emphasis on quality of research and research products.
- A need to aggressively exploit delegated authorities to improve management of research resources.

June '83 The Station investigates the benefits of tying into FLIPS (Forest Level Information Planning System), an agencywide computerized information storage and retrieval system.

A newly formed Word Processing Committee reports that the IBM Personal Computer is essentially the same as the Displaywriter now being used, but only costs roughly 1/5 as much.

Director Loveless announces a major reorganization of Station research in Arizona, resulting in four new projects from five existing ones:
- Seedling Physiology   Flagstaff. Dick Tinus, Project Leader
- Management of Ponderosa Pine, Mixed Conifers, and Pinyon-juniper Ecosystems of the Southwest   Flagstaff. Frank Ronco, Project Leader
- Management of Southwest Watersheds Tempe. Len DeBano, Project Leader
- Range, Wildlife, and Fish Habitat Research in the Southwest   Tempe. Dave Patton, Project Leader

November '83 – The threatened Avalanche Warning Center has new life   to be partly sponsored by the Colorado Department of Natural Resources.

January '84 Harold Coley comes on board from the WO as Assistant Director for Research Support Services, vice Jackie Cables.

A special issue of the Station Newsletter, the *Rocky Mountain Update*, is devoted to FLIPS — the Forest Level Information Processing System — and the Data General workstations will soon render most typewriters obsolete.

Dave Garrett, past Beaver Creek Project Leader, returns to Flagstaff as Dean of the NAU Forestry School.

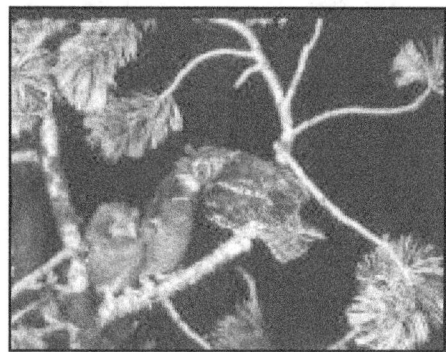

A flammulated owl feeds a moth to one of her young on the Manitou Experimental Forest, Colorado. Brian Linkhart and Richard Reynolds have the longest running study ever on this diminutive owl's behavior, habitat requirements, and territorial size.

April '84   The Publications Control Committee is still struggling to minimize delays in printing Station publications resulting from President Reagan's moratorium on government publishing.

May '84   Scientist Art Judson (Fort Collins) receives the Outstanding Publication Award for 1983.

July '84   Marty Raphael comes to Laramie as Project Leader for "Effects of Multiple-use Land Management on Wildlife in the Central Rocky Mountains."

Nineteen foresters from 12 nations visit the Flagstaff lab as part of an international forestry workshop on arid environments at the University of Arizona.

Zheng Quan Li, a forestry engineer from the People's Republic of China, is spending a year in the Multiresource Inventory Techniques project, with Hans Schreuder.

November '84   Seven of 10 Research Highlights submitted by the Station are accepted for the Chief's annual Research Accomplishments Report.

Scientist Bev Driver (Fort Collins) is elected a Fellow of the Academy of Leisure Sciences.

December '84   The Station's Civil Rights Committee announces that the Station met or exceeded all its goals in several hiring categories.

January '85   The new Rolm telephone system goes on stream. Calls no longer need go through a switchboard, and we have call-forwarding, call-waiting and conference calling.

February '85   The Rocky Mountain Station, Region 3, and the Secretaria de Agricultura y Recursos Hidraulicos hold a conference on Management and Utilization of Arid Land Plants in Saltillo, Mexico, as part of a continuing cross-border scientific exchange.

March '85   Charlie Loveless's Director's Corner again emphasizes the importance of maintaining physical fitness: "Come sweat with me!"

Charlie is recognized as "Outstanding Alumnus" by the University of Florida's School of Forestry and Conservation, an award only presented twice before.

Project Leader Ardell Bjugstad (Rapid City) receives the Station's first Civil Rights Award.

May '85   A new Data General MV 8000 with four megabytes of memory is installed at Station headquarters.

June '85   The Station's first smoking (or *non-smoking*) policy is issued.

July '85   RM Station celebrates its 50th anniversary! An elaborate Open House takes the efforts of almost everyone in Station Headquarters. Assistant Director Clyde Fasick and his committee run the show.

Station scientists also play a major role in the annual meeting of the Society of American Foresters, at CSU this year, overlapping our anniversary celebration.

Elbert Little, 77-year-old retired Chief Dendrologist for the Forest Service, returns to his old haunts around Flagstaff to work as a volunteer with Frank Ronco and Jerry Gottfried. Little picked up on a study of pinyon phenology he started nearly 50 years ago.

September '85   Scientist Debbie Finch, Laramie, receives the 1984 Outstanding Publication Award.

November '85   Scientist Bev Driver (Fort Collins) receives the Theodore and Franklin Roosevelt award for excellence in Recreation and Park Research, from the National Recreation and Park Association.

January '86   Retirements take a toll on Station scientists and Project Leaders: Duane Knipe, Range Scientist at Tempe; Dave Patton, Wildlife Biologist and Project Leader, Tempe; Ron Tabler, Hydrologist and Project Leader, Laramie; Lorin Ward, Wildlife Biologist, Laramie.

March '86   About 125 employees, including several Project Leaders from field labs, hear Director Loveless frankly discuss austere FY 86, 87, and 88 budget projections and their implications.

Kieth Severson is the new leader for the wildlife project in Tempe, vice Dave Patton.

The Directorate and Management Team develop Vision and Mission statements to formalize the Station's research and management philosophies.

WESTFORNET evolves to FS INFO as the package of library and information retrieval services continues to spread east, and goes national.

April '86   Computer Specialist Clarence Adair and Personnel Specialist Wil Dixon (Fort Collins) arrange a potluck luncheon as part of Black History Month prior to a meeting of the Station's Civil Rights Committee.

June '86   Dixie Smith, Station Deputy Director for the past 11 years, retires after a lengthy Federal career as Rangeland Scientist and research administrator.

Jim McCallum is the new computer specialist working on the Data General equipment.

August '86   Along with a new mission for the Fort Collins Insect and Disease project comes a new Project Leader, Charles (Terry) Shaw III. Frank Hawksworth steps down as PL, but stays on as Research Plant Pathologist.

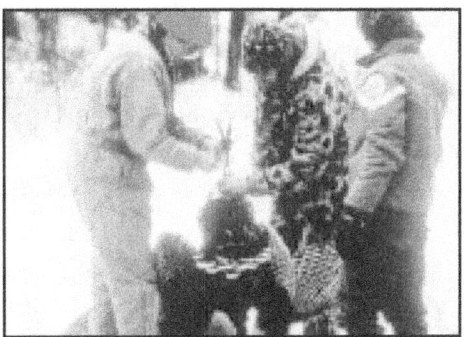

No, it's not for Thanksgiving dinner! Mark Rumble (left) and crew band and evaluate the condition of a Merriam's turkey, a species now expanding its range in the Black Hills of South Dakota.

Forest Fire and Atmospheric Science Research is reorganized nationally. The fire project at Flagstaff closes and personnel are transferred to the Pacific Southwest Station and the Atmospheric Deposition unit at Fort Collins.

RM Station is working with The Nature Conservancy to finalize designation of 28 Research Natural Areas in the Southwest.

September '86   About 40 people enjoy a program and bueno potluck lunch in celebration of National Hispanic Heritage Week at Station headquarters.

October '86   Editor Bob Winokur (Fort Collins) inaugurates innovative use of the DG system to electronically compile proceedings of a symposium, the first such use in the Forest Service.

December '86   Computer Specialist Jim McCallum and Clarence Adair (Fort Collins) install the Station's new Data General MV 10,000 mainframe computer.

January '87   Director Loveless says 1986 was a banner year for the RM Station. Sixty-three scientists in 15 work units produced 252 scientific publications, the highest number ever at the Station, and with a significantly reduced staff.

March '87   Stephen McDonald is new Assistant Director for Research   North, replacing Clyde Fasick, who has transferred to the WO.

The Directorate, Project Leaders, and Group Leaders spend 3 days at Rio Rico in southern Arizona focusing on "Expanding the Research Perspective." The meeting ends with a field trip to the Santa Rita Experiment Range.

June '87   A committee of scientists (Frank Vertucci, R. A. Schmidt, Brian Geils, and Merrill Kaufmann) is appointed to assess the laboratory space and equipment situation at Fort Collins.

About 50 Station retirees and their spouses attend a luncheon in their honor in Fort Collins.

July '87   "Management of Subalpine Forests: Building on 50 Years of Research" is the theme as Fraser Experimental Forest celebrates its 50th anniversary. About 130 scientists and managers participate in the technical conference in nearby Silver Creek. Scientist Chuck Troendle (Fort Collins) is organizer.

September '87   Eighteen members of the Forest Insect and Disease Staff, WO, come to RM Station for a Technical Assistance Visit. All Station units with FIDR responsibilities are involved.

October '87   Scientist Frank Hawksworth (Fort Collins) is keynote speaker at the National Symposium on Forest Entomology and Pathology in Durango, Mexico. Rumor is Frank generated mucho laughs   he gave his presentation in Spanish.

November '87   Scientist John Hof (Fort Collins) receives the Outstanding Research Publication Award for 1986.

December '87   Director Loveless ticks off some highlights of 1987:

- Our Station scientists publish a new high of over 260 technical papers.
- The Fraser 50-year anniversary symposium and rededication.
- Our frequency rates for vehicle accidents and personal injuries are cut in half from last year.
- We met our FY 87 targets for hiring women and minorities.

The Station gets hints that the Santa Rita Experimental Range and the Tempe Forestry Sciences Lab are on the negotiating block in a complex series of Federal/State land swaps in Arizona.

The Laramie lab holds an open house to celebrate 25 years of research. Over 200 attend.

January '88   Two mobile trailers along the east side of the parking lot behind the Fort Collins Headquarters building will provide needed space, one for atmospheric deposition researchers, the other for maintenance personnel.

February '88   A joint decision announced by the Forest Service, Arizona State University, and Northern Arizona University confirms the move: Station research at Tempe will be relocated to Flagstaff. ASU wants to build a $25 million Goldwater Center for Science and Engineering on the Tempe site. The move is at least 3 to 5 years away.

June '88 Project Manager Wayne White and Sue Janzen (Administrative Services), Fort Collins, receive a 1988 USDA Honor Award for developing the Automated Purchase Order system (APOS) now being used nationwide.

Station Scientist Dan Uresk takes over Project Leader duties at Rapid City so Ardell Bjugstad can devote more time to research and special assignments.

December '88 Scientist Chuck Troendle (Fort Collins) is selected to receive the 1987 Outstanding Research Publication Award.

January '89 A revised smoking policy stipulates the Break Room at Headquarters will be smoke-free.

March '89 Strategic planning is the dominant theme of the Station's 1989 Management Team meeting in Fort Collins. A draft plan for RM Station is being synthesized from information generated by six small groups. Earl Aldon, George Peterson, and Bob Hamre should have a draft ready by May 1.

Bob Winokur, Station editor, is selected Mayor of Fort Collins by the City Council. "Trapper" has been a Councilman since 1987.

May '89 Station Librarian Frances Barney is honored with a specially engraved plaque by Station scientists in a surprise ceremony.

June '89 Charlie Loveless retires after nearly 40 years as a professional in natural resources, the last 8 as Director at RM Station.

Jim McCallum, Computer Specialist in Fort Collins, reports that the Forest Service has purchased the new Oracle Relational Data Base Management System, which "will give us the power we didn't have before to integrate data and share information."

Project Leaders Marty Raphael, Laramie, and Len Ruggiero, Pacific Northwest Research Station, trade places.

Glenn Peterson, Lincoln, evaluates Dothistroma pini *on Austrian pine on the Horning Farm experimental area.*

October '89 Hank Montrey comes from the Forest Products Lab in Madison to be the Station's eighth Director.

Fire causes considerable damage to a Station building adjacent to the Rapid City lab; much research equipment inside is destroyed.

Project Leader Doug Fox's (Fort Collins) Atmospheric Deposition Research unit is broadened to Effects of Atmospheric Change on Alpine and Subalpine Forest Ecosystems as part of the U.S. Global Change Research Program.

A Fisheries Habitat Research Team is established as part of Laramie's Wildlife Habitat unit.

December '89 Director Montrey convenes a major, 3-day Management Team retreat at CSU, where participants develop a three-element Vision Statement and a series of eight Organizational Commitments to serve as guiding principles for all our organizational and personal statements, decisions, and actions.

January '90 George Peterson and Bev Driver (Fort Collins) receive, as a team, a Superior Scientist Award for their research in "valuing public amenity goods and services."

February '90 With 3.6 publications per scientist year, Rocky Mountain and Southeastern Stations share the lead in productivity last year.

Fort Collins scientists Tom Brown and John Hof receive the Outstanding Research Publication Awards for 1988 an 1989, respectively.

The 1990 spending bill for Interior and Related Agencies earmarks $1.5 million for planning the combined RM/NAU Forestry Sciences Complex at Flagstaff. Wayne White is detailed to the Director's staff to handle planning.

April '90 Tom Hoekstra, arriving from the North Central Station, becomes new Assistant Director for Planning and Applications.

Joe Mitchell comes on board at Rapid City as Native American Liaison. This is a pilot effort for the Forest Service.

June '90 A 4-day strategic planning session in Fort Collins focuses on understanding and packaging our current and projected research programs, and the decisionmaking criteria that should be used to make future program adjustments.

July '90 RM Station will play a major role in the next national RPA Assessment, a congressionally mandated projection of future supply and demand for all forest and rangeland resources. Our scientists will author many sections, and Publications will edit, print, and distribute the reports.

Scientist Frank Hawksworth (Fort Collins) receives the Chief's Award for Excellence in Technology Transfer for 1989, for over 40 years of research on dwarf mistletoes.

Three scientists from La Madera Experiment Station in Chihuahua, Mexico, come to the Tempe lab to learn about our research on fire effects and erosional processes.

GLEES (Glacier Lakes Ecosystem Experiments Site) in southern Wyoming is host to several students from Howard University in Washington, D.C. The week-long program introduces minority students to a broad range of Forest Service research efforts.

September '90 Station Director Hank Montrey selects Larry Sandoval (Technician at Flagstaff) to be the Station's Innovation Coordinator, heading up Project 3E (energy, excellence, empowerment). Larry's task is to coordinate the stimulation, evaluation, and implementation of RM employee ideas for improving the Station and adding value to what we do.

December '90 To focus responsibility for research data management in one administrative unit, the Leadership Team establishes Biometrics and Research Data Systems, to be led by Biometrician Rudy King (Fort Collins). BARDS will cover biometrics support, systems analysis and computer programming analysis, management and protection of Station research data and long-term data bases, and development and support of the Station's GIS strategy.

John Rinne, Fisheries Biologist at Tempe, goes international, participating in conferences on rare fish in England and Japan this past year, and in Greece next year.

January '91 Range Scientist John Mitchell (Fort Collins) pilots a Huey medical evacuation helicopter on night missions in Kuwait during the brief Gulf War.

Ned Nikolov arrives from Bulgaria to work with the Effects of Atmospheric Change project, Fort Collins.

March '91   Rocky Mountain Station (primarily Chuck Troendle) assists the Department of Justice in the rebuttal portion of Colorado Water Division I Reserved Water Rights Case. (This effort led to the establishment of the Stream Team the following year.)

April '91   Director Montrey announces Tom Hoekstra will assume duties as both Assistant Director for Research North and Acting Assistant Director for Research South. Marcia Patton-Mallory comes from the WO as Assistant Director for Planning and Applications.

Anna Schoettle examines white pine blister rust on a western white pine. (photo credit: D. Croswell)

Additional leadership changes: Carl Edminster is Acting Project Leader for the Multiresource Unit at Fort Collins, Doug Fox is Acting Program Manager for the Interior West Global Change RD&A at Fort Collins, Chuck Troendle is Project Leader developing an integrated Watershed/Fisheries unit at Laramie, and Bob Musselman is Acting Project Leader for Effects of Atmospheric Change.

Debbie Finch, Wildlife Research Biologist at Laramie, is chosen to coordinate the new interagency, international Neotropical Migratory Bird Conservation program, Partners in Flight. She will be on assignment to the WO for 1 or 2 years.

May '91   Ground is broken for the new $21.5 million Southwest Forestry Sciences Complex on the NAU campus. This is the first Federal/State partnership of its kind in the nation.

Rocky Boyd returns to the Station from the WO as Operations Group Leader.

June '91   The new building being constructed in the back of the Headquarters parking lot will be home for procurement, budget, and fiscal employees.

August '91   Can sewage sludge improve water quality? Soil Scientist Richard Aguilar, Albuquerque, receives a grant from the New Mexico Water Resources Research Institute to study the effects of sewage sludge on vegetation and water quality in a semiarid environment.

December '91   Michele Schoeneberger is Acting Project Leader for Improvement of Stress and Pest Resistance of Great Plains Tree Species in Lincoln vice Bill Rietveld, who becomes Director of the Center for Semiarid Agroforestry.

February '92   Range scientist Linda Joyce and Project Leader John Hof (Fort Collins) again receive Outstanding Research Publication Awards for 1990 and 1991, respectively.

Scientist Bev Driver, Fort Collins, is installed as President of the Academy of Leisure Sciences.

John Hof, Fort Collins, is selected as one of three FS scientists to receive a Superior Science Award.

June '92 Project Leader Earl Aldon (Albuquerque) joins the exclusive club of GM-15 scientists via the panel evaluation process in the Chief's Office. Other GM-15s at the Station include Tom Hoekstra, George Peterson, Doug Fox, Hans Schreuder, John Hof, Bev Driver, and Len DeBano. *Peterson went on to become the Station's first GS-16 scientist. Linda Joyce and Karen Clancy became the Station's first female GM-15 scientists in 1999.*

Larry Schmidt comes to Fort Collins from the WO to lead the Station's new Stream Systems Technology Center, better known as the "Stream Team."

September '92 Denver Burns becomes the Station's ninth Director, succeeding Hank Montrey, who is moving to the WO. Denver comes from the Northeastern Station.

Michele Shoeneberger is now the official Project Leader for Improvement of Stress and Pest Resistance of Great Plains Tree Species in Lincoln.

November '92 Project Leader Dan Uresk, Rapid City, is nominated for the Chief's Award for Excellence in Technology Transfer for his creation of an ecological classification and monitoring system for rangeland resources.

Scientists Terry Shaw and Wil Moir, Fort Collins, receive a Chief's Award from F. Dale Robertson for Leadership in New Perspectives for successfully applying all four principles of the New Perspectives concept to their recent project on Integrated Pest Management and Timber Sales.

January '93 TERRA, the Terrestrial Ecosystems Regional Research and Analysis laboratory (Doug Fox, leader), celebrates its beginning with an open house at its new facility on Oak Street in Fort Collins. TERRA is a joint effort by USDA and USDI to integrate multidisciplinary ecosystem research projects within the US Global Change Research Program.

February '93 Burchard Heede, Hydrologist at Tempe, receives the Chief's Distinguished Scientist Award.

Don Reichert, Forestry Technician at Fort Collins, is elected National Secretary/Treasurer for the National Federation of Federal Employees in Washington, DC. Don is taking a 2-year leave of absence from the Station.

March '93 The *RM Update* newsletter initiates a "Temporary Topics" column as a forum for concerns of temporary employees.

Project Leader Dan Uresk, Rapid City, and Station Biometrician Rudy King, Fort Collins, are part of a Station/Region research team selected to receive the "Chief's Leadership in New Perspectives Award."

May '93 The Southwest Forest Science Complex in Flagstaff is formally dedicated. The "technical side" of the dedication will culminate with a Conference on Sustainable Ecological Systems in July.

Linda Joyce becomes Project Leader for Sustaining Alpine and Forest Ecosystems Under Atmospheric and Terrestrial Disturbances, Fort Collins.

July '93 Clarence Adair (Fort Collins) is appointed to the new position of Civil Rights Director for the Station.

Joe Tainter starts as Project Leader for the new Cultural Heritage unit at Albuquerque.

August '93 Joe Mitchell, Native American Educational Liason, moves from Rapid City to Fort Collins as the program is expanded to a national focus.

October '93 INT and RM Leadership Teams meet in Ogden to discuss a proposed merger of the two Stations.

First issue of the Station's weekly internal newsletter, *Director's Notes*, is published. Rick Fletcher is editor.

November '93   Forest Service Chief Dale Robertson appoints RM Station Director Denver Burns as Acting Director, Intermountain Station.

Debbie Finch is appointed Project Leader for Sustainability of Southwestern Grassland Watersheds, Albuquerque.

Dan Neary is appointed Project Leader for Management of Southwestern Watersheds, Flagstaff.

Director Burns presents a proposal for an inter-agency Natural Resources Research Center in Fort Collins to Assistant Agriculture Secretary Wardell Thompson.

December '93   The RM Technicians Workshop in Denver gives these members of the research team an opportunity to exchange "how-to-do-it" ideas.

January '94   Peg Harris comes from the Northeast Station as Acting Assistant Director for Planning and Applications, filling in for Marcia Patton-Mallory.

Feb. '94   RM Station is one of the pilot units in Project 615, the working title for the new telecommunications system being designed to replace the Data General system.

Linda Joyce, Program Leader in Fort Collins, plays a major role in the Society for Range Management annual meeting in Colorado Springs, where she receives an Outstanding Achievement Award for advancing the art and science of range management.

March '94   The RM/INT Management Team meeting in Albuquerque is a "shot in the arm" for moving the two Stations toward merger.

Director Burns appoints Project Leaders Terry Shaw, Len Ruggiero, George Peterson, and Debbie Finch to an innovative effort to increase Project Leader participation in decisionmaking.

May '94   Harold Coley and Peg Harris pick up some Acting duties at INT to ensure that administrative activities for both RM and INT proceed as normal after the recent "buyout" (paid early retirement program).

June '94   Seven students from 1890 Historically Black Colleges are spending their summer working with RM scientists.

July '94   Dave Kimbrough, Intermountain Station, is named Facilities Manager for RM and INT; he will also serve as Project Manager for the Natural Resources Research Center.

Angela Chavez is now officially our Director of Computer Systems. She comes from the Southern Region.

August '94   The Albuquerque unit receives both regional and national EPA awards for its research on developing ways to improve rangelands by applying sewage sludge.

RBAIS is an acronym for the new Research Budget and Attainment Information System software being developed to replace the outmoded RAR (Research Attainment Report). Glen Brink will oversee development at RM and is instrumental in developing the system for Research.

A trial with the "Charged-as-Worked" accounting system, where the cost of a job or service is assigned to the benefiting RWU, shows the task isn't easy.

September '94   The Management Team spends two days evaluating various participative management experiments tried over the past several months.

Assistant Director Tom Hoekstra says our collaborative research with INIFAP (Mexico's counterpart to FS Research) extends literally from A to Z: Agroforestry to Zenaida doves. Celedonio Aguirre-Bravo is the major facilitating force between RM and INIFAP. The Station is printing a directory containing over 700 names of US and Mexican scientists and 5,000 keywords in English and Spanish for easy reference.

RM hosts the Second Annual Fraser Experimental Forest Natural Resources Career Camp for 20 Hispanic high school students. Technicians Manual Martinez and Steve Mata lead the effort.

October '94   RM Station produces 311 publications in FY 94, according to the new Research Attainment Report, an average of about five per scientist.

Scientist Bev Driver (Fort Collins) receives the Agency's Distinguished Science Award for 1994 for sustained scientific contributions to improve management of outdoor recreation resources.

November '94   Dick Tinus, Flagstaff, takes over the Global Change Program vice Linda Joyce, who is stepping down.

December '94   Harold Coley retires as Assistant Director for Administration.

Scientist Brian Kent (Fort Collins) is selected to be Acting Assistant Director for Research, with responsibility for research units in Fort Collins and Laramie. John Hof will fill in as Acting Project Leader behind Brian.

January '95   Project Leader Terry Shaw (Fort Collins) accepts a 2-year detail with R-10 in Alaska. Brian Geils will be Acting Project Leader.

The name of our Center for Semiarid Agroforestry in Lincoln is now officially the National Agroforestry Center to reflect its national and international basis.

Measuring water content of the snow pack on Willow Creek, White Mountain Watersheds, Arizona.

Jim Haskell, arriving from USDA, begins a 120-day detail as Assistant Director for Administration.

April '95   The Center for Great Plains Ecosystem Research is created at Rapid City, with Dan Uresk as Program Leader.

The Natural Resource Conservation Service assigns three people to our National Agroforestry Center, Lincoln.

June '95   The Rapid City lab is recognized by the Forest Service for its research on the black-tailed prairie dog as a keystone species supporting such rare species as the black-footed ferret, swift fox, and burrowing owl.

July '95   Driving less but crashing more   seems to be the pattern with chargeable motor vehicle accidents this year.

August '95   Proposed significant budget cuts have employees worrying about downsizing, furloughs and reductions-in-force. The proposed merger of RM and INT should not be affected, however.

Project 615 equipment is installed at Fort Collins; it should be operational in September.

October '95   The Interior West Global Change Program is terminated due to lack of funding.

November '95   Project Leader Linda Joyce, Fort Collins, earns a Forest Service Superior Scientist Award.

The National Agroforestry Center, Lincoln, is now a joint venture with the USDA Natural Resources Conservation Service. A new RWU description is being developed.

December '95   Project Leader Joe Tainter, Albuquerque, helps organize Environmental Dimensions of Cultural Conflict, a unique conference focused on the potential for violence between peoples of different cultures.

The RM/INT Leadership Team meeting focuses on ways the Stations could integrate key operations when the merger becomes final.

Marcia Patton-Mallory returns to her post as Assistant Director for Planning and Applications. She will also be Acting Assistant Director for Administration.

January '96   Station employees return to work after a two-week furlough forced by a Congressional impasse on the Federal budget.

Technology Transfer Program Leader Jerry Bratton reports the National Agroforestry Center in Lincoln has cost-shared 45 demonstration/application projects and 10 assessment projects over the past 4 years.

February '96   Tom Swetnam, Laboratory of Tree-Ring Research, University of Arizona, starts a 3-month sabbatical at RM Headquarters studying fire, insect, and other disturbance histories in forests.

May '96   Marcia Patton-Mallory and Brian Kent are selected for 1-year details as Assistant Directors for Research. Jim Haskell returns to RM as Assistant Director for Administration. Marcia and Brian will share Planning and Applications AD duties.

The RM Station Management Team meets for a week in Fort Collins.

June '96   Director Burns announces realignment of Research Work Units: Flagstaff (4152, 4251, 4302), Fort Collins (4803, 4851, 4852), and Rapid City (4252) report to AD Marcia Patton-Mallory. Albuquerque (4351, 4853), Fort Collins (4802), and EM units 4651, 4652, 4653 report to AD Brian Kent. Biometrics and Information Management report to Marcia. The Stream Team and National Agroforestry Center report directly to Denver. Brian has Planning.

The INT Leadership Team is now participating in RM staff briefings, via conference call.

August '96   The General Services Administration and Colorado State University wrap up negotiations on land south of Prospect Road for the Natural Resources Research Center.

September '96   Thieves break into the Albuquerque lab, stealing much computer equipment.

Octcober '96   RM Station hosts the Researchwide Assistant Directors' and Program Managers' meeting, in Fort Collins. Major emphasis is on making the science/management partnership work.

November '96   A Departmentwide moratorium on purchase of "information technology products" freezes Project 615.

January '97   A joint RM/INT Leadership team meeting in Fort Collins concentrates on joint research priorities and budget strategies.

Regional Foresters from Regions 1, 2, 3, and 4 meet with the RM/INT Leadership team to coordinate joint research/management efforts.

Carol Klopatek, Microbial Ecologist at Flagstaff, reports on the unique National Below Ground Sustainability Workshop she headed last fall in Washington, DC: how to preserve organisms and processes below ground that sustain forest ecosystems.

Studies at Rapid City showed that the swift fox relied on prairie dogs for half its diet.

February '97   Over 20 people participate in the Technical Assistance Visit with Karen Clancy's Impacts of Ecological Disturbances on Southwestern Conifers project, Flagstaff.

March '97   Project Leader Debbie Finch, Albuquerque, and Scientist John Rinne, Flagstaff, are technical advisors to Region 3 teams working to protect threatened and endangered birds and fish.

Todd Mowrer, Research Forester at Fort Collins, Joe Ganey, Wildlife Biologist at Flagstaff, and Dan Uresk, Wildlife Biologist at Rapid City, receive awards from their professional organizations.

April '97   Down-sizing continues: from October 1992 through February 1997, Forest Service Research employment has dropped from 2,628 to 1,989.

Station headquarters relocated to the new Natural Resources Research Center in 2000.

May '97   It's official! The Washington Office says the Rocky Mountain Forest and Range Experiment Station and the Intermountain Research Station are now one entity: the Rocky Mountain Research Station. *(Station headquarters moved into the National Resources Research Center [NRRC] in Fort Collins in 2000.)*

1997 Station Organization Chart (Prior to Merger)

Station Director
Denver Burns

**Stream Systems
Technology Center**
Larry Schmidt

**Assistant Director
for Research**
Marcia Patton-Mallory
(Acting)

**Assistant Director
for Research**
Brian Kent (Acting)

**Assistant Director
for Administration**
Jim Haskell

**Impacts of Ecological
Disturbances/ W. Conifer**
RWU-4152
Karen Clancy

**Fish & Watersheds
Aquatic/Riparian Ecosystems**
RWU-4352
Charles Troendle

Computer Systems
Angela Chavez

**Sustainability of SW
Forests & Woodlands**
RWU-4251
Bill Block

**Soils, Plants, Animals,
Humans/Rio Grande Basin**
RWU-4652
Deborah Finch

Personnel & Civil Rights
Shari Blakey

**Ecosystems/Northern &
Central Plains**
RWU-4252
Daniel Uresk

**Cultural Heritage
Research/SW**
RWU-4853
Joseph Tainter

Facilities Management
David Kimbrough

**Sustaining Riparian
Systems in SW Forests**
RWU-4302
Daniel Neary

**SW Grassland &
Riparian Ecosystems**
RWU-4351
Deborah Finch

Management Analyst
Wilbert Boyd

**Resource Analysis
Research**
RWU-4803
John Hof

**Atmospheric & Terrestrial
Disturbances on Ecosystems**
RWU-4451
Linda Joyce

Administrative Services
Susan Janzen

**Valuation of Wildland
Resource Benefits**
RWU-4851
George Peterson

**Ecosystem Management in
Borderlands of the SW**
RWU-4651
Carleton Edminster

Budget & Finance
Harold Kehr

**Nat. Resource Assessment
Ecology & Management**
RWU-4852
John Hof (Acting)

**Soc., Bio., and Physical
Comp./CO Front Range**
RWU-4653
Brian Kent

**Safety, Health, &
Environment**
Mike Anderson

Biometrics
Rudy King

**Resource Inventory
Techniques**
RWU-4802
Raymond Czaplewski

**Cooperative Agency
Saving U**
Don Reichert

Publications
Land Eskew

**National Agroforestry
Center**
Willis Rietveld

Library
Frances Barney

**Tree based Buffer Strips
Technology**
RWU-4551
Michele Schoeneberger

Public Affairs
Rick Fletcher

The first Management Team meeting of the newly formed Rocky Mountain Research Station: Ogden, Utah, 1997.
1. Bill Block, Flagstaff 2. Don Latham, Missoula 3. Karen Clancy, Flagstaff 4. Mark Hutchins, Ogden 5. Robin Tausch, Reno 6. Larry Schmidt, Fort Collins 7. Louise Kingsbury, Ogden 8. Richard Krebill, Ogden 9. Mike Anderson, Fort Collins 10. Patrick Corts, Missoula 11. Dennis Ferguson, Moscow 12. Dan Neary, Flagstaff 13. Shary Kennedy, Rapid City 14. Shari Blakey, Fort Collins 15. Chuck Troendle, Fort Collins 16. Warren Clary, Boise 17. Ward McCaughey, Bozeman 18. Michael Williams, Fort Collins 19. Lane Eskew, Fort Collins 20. Carl Edminster, Flagstaff 21. George Peterson, Fort Collins 22. William Elliot, Moscow 23. Jesse Logan, Logan 24. Andy Lawrence, Moscow 25. Durant McArthur, Provo 26. Barbi Rate, Ogden 27. Dristen Stuart Lincoln 28. Karen Charlton, Ogden 29. Lori Kelly, Laramie 30. John Hof, Fort Collins 31. Debbie Finch, Albuquerque 32. Dwane Van Hooser, Ogden 33. Brian Kent, Fort Collins 34. Linda Joyce, Fort Collins 35. Michele Schoeneberger, Lincoln 36. Jim Haskell, Fort Collins 37. Carol Ayer, Ogden 38. JoAn Steele, Ogden 39. Martha Pforr, Fort Collins 40. Maurine Stettler, Ogden 41. Pat Ford, Provo 42. Cecelia Johnson, Missoula 43. Harold Kehr, Fort Collins 44. Angie Evendon, Missoula 45. Keith Evans, Ogden 46. Rudy King, Fort Collins 47. Erv Schuster, Missoula 48. Chuck Fierro, Ogden 49. Marcia Patton Mallory, Fort Collins 50. Dean Knighton, Ogden 51. Raymond Brown, Logan 52. Tamara Hanan, Ogden 53. Russell Graham, Moscow 54. Carmen Gallegos, Albuquerque 55. Linda Baer, Logan 56. Denver Burns, Fort Collins 57. Leslie Parrott, Boise 58. Vicki Berrett, Ogden 59. Darold Ward, Missoula 60. Kevin Ryan, Missoula 61. Alan Harvey, Moscow 62. David Parsons, Missoula 63. Elaine Poser, Odgen 64. Dan Uresk, Rapid City 65. Len Ruggiero, Missoula 66. David Tippets, Ogden.

A Few Significant Publications

Aguirre-Bravo, Celedonio; Eskew, Lane; Gonzalez,-Vicente, Carlos; Villa-Salas, Avalino B.; technical editors/compilers. 1995. *Partnerships for Sustainable Forest Ecosystem Management: Fifth Mexico/US Biennial Symposium.* 1994 October 17-20, Guadalajara, Jalisco, Mexico. General Technical Report RM-GTR-266. Fort Collins, CO: U.S. Department of Agriculture, Forest Service, Rocky Mountain Forest and Range Experiment Station. 201 p. (English), 218 p. (Spanish).

Alexander, Robert R.; Edminster, Carleton B. 1980. *Management of Spruce-fir in Even-aged Stands in the Central Rocky Mountains.* Research Paper RM-217. Fort Collins, CO: U.S. Department of Agriculture, Forest Service, Rocky Mountain Forest and Range Experiment Station. 14 p.

Block, W.M.; Finch, D.M., technical editors. 1997. *Songbird Ecology in Southwestern Ponderosa Pine Forests: a Literature Review.* General Technical Report RM-GTR-292. Fort Collins, CO: U.S. Department of Agriculture, Forest Service, Rocky Mountain Forest and Range Experiment Station. 152 p.

Brown, Thomas C.; Binkley, Dan. 1994. *Effect of Management on Water Quality in North American Forests.* General Technical Report RM-248. Fort Collins, CO: U.S. Department of Agriculture, Forest Service, Rocky Mountain Forest and Range Experiment Station. 27 p.

Brown, T.C.; Harding, B.L.; Payton, E.A. 1990. *Marginal Economic Value of Streamflow: a Case Study for the Colorado River Basin. Water Resources Research* 26(12): 2845-2859.

Covington, Wallace W.; DeBano, Leonard F. (technical coordinators). 1994. *Sustainable Ecological Systems: Implementing an Ecological Approach to Land Management.* 1993 July 12-15; Flagstaff, AZ. General Technical Report RM-247. Fort Collins CO: U.S. Department of Agriculture,

Forest Service, Rocky Mountain Forest and Range Experiment Station. 363 p.

Currie, Pat O. 1975. *Grazing Management of Ponderosa Pine-bunchgrass Ranges of the Central Rocky Mountains: the Status of Our Knowledge.* Research Paper RM-159. Fort Collins, CO: U.S. Department of Agriculture, Forest Service, Rocky Mountain Forest and Range Experiment Station. 24 p.

Daniel, Terry C.; Boster, Ron. S. 1976. *Measuring Landscape Esthetics: the Scenic Beauty Estimation Method.* Research Paper RM-167. Fort Collins, CO: U.S. Department of Agriculture, Forest Service, Rocky Mountain Forest and Range Experiment Station. 66 p.

DeBano, Leonard F.; Ffolliott, Peter F.; Ortega-Rubio, Alfredo; and others, technical coordinators. 1995. *Biodiversity and Management of the Madrean Archipelago: the Sky Islands of Southwestern United States and Northwestern Mexico.* 1994 Sept. 19-23; Tucson, AZ. General Technical Report RM-GTR-264. Fort Collins, CO: U.S. Department of Agriculture, Forest Service, Rocky Mountain Forest and Range Experiment Station. 669 p.

DeByle, Norbert V.; Winokur, Robert P., editors. 1985. *Aspen: Ecology and Management in the Western United States.* General Technical Report RM-119. Fort Collins, CO: U.S. Department of Agriculture, Forest Service, Rocky Mountain Forest and Range Experiment Station. 283 p.

Driver, B.; Brown, P.; Gregoire, T.; Stankey, G. 1987. *The ROS Planning System: Evolution, Basic Concepts, and Research Needed. Leisure Sciences* 9(3):203-214.

Driver, B.; Brown, P.; Peterson, G., editors. 1991. *Benefits of Leisure.* State College, PA: Venture Publishing. 484 p.

Driver, B.L.; Dustin, Daniel; Baltic, Tony; Elsner, Gary; Peterson, G.L. (editors). 1996. *Nature and the Human Spirit: Toward an Expanded Land Management Ethic.* College Station, PA: Venture Publishing, Inc. 488 p.

Flather, Curtis H.; Hoekstra, Thomas W. 1989. *An Analysis of the Wildlife and Fish Situation in the United States: 1989   2140.* General Technical Report RM-178. Fort Collins, CO: U.S. Department of Agriculture, Forest Service, Rocky Mountain Forest and Range Experiment Station. 147 p.

Flather, Curtis H.; Joyce, Linda A.; Bloomgarden, Carol A. 1994. *Species Endangerment Patterns in the United States.* General Technical Report RM-241. Fort Collins, CO: U.S. Department of Agriculture, Forest Service, Rocky Mountain Forest and Range Experiment Station. 42 p.

Gary, Howard L. 1985. *A Summary of Research at the Manitou Experimental Forest in Colorado, 1937-1983.* General Technical Report RM-116. Fort Collins, CO: U.S. Department of Agriculture, Forest Service, Rocky Mountain Forest and Range Experiment Station. 24 p.

Gillilan, D.M.; Brown, T.C. 1997. *Instream Flow Protection: Seeking a Balance in Western Water Use.* Island Press, Wash. D.C. 417 p.

Hawksworth, Frank G.; Wiens, Delbert. 1996. *Dwarf Mistletoes: Biology, Pathology, and Systematics.* Agriculture Handbook 709. Washington, DC: U.S. Department of Agriculture, Forest Service. 410 p.

Heede, Burchard H. 1976. *Gully Development and Control: the Status of Our Knowledge.* Research Paper RM-169. Fort Collins, CO: U.S. Department of Agriculture, Forest Service, Rocky Mountain Forest and Range Experiment Station, 42 p.

Hof, John G.; Lee, Robert D.; Dyer, A. Allen; Kent, Brian M. 1985. *An Analysis of Joint Costs in a Managed Forest Ecosystem. Journal of Environmental Economics and Management.* 12: 338-352.

Joyce, Linda A. 1989. *An Analysis of the Range Forage Situation in the United States, 1989-2040: a Technical Document Supporting the 1989 USDA Forest Service RPA Assessment.* General Technical Report RM-180. Fort Collins, CO: U.S. Department of Agriculture, Forest Service, Rocky Mountain Forest and Range Experiment Station. 136 p.

Joyce, Linda A.; Fosberg, Michael A.; Comanor, Joan M. 1990. *Climate Change and America's Forests.* General Technical Report RM-187. Fort Collins, CO: U.S. Department of Agriculture, Forest Service, Rocky Mountain Forest and Range Experiment Station. 12 p.

Judson, Arthur; King, Rudy M.; Brink, Glen E. 1986. *Multi-basin Avalanche Simulation: a Model. Cold Regions Science and Technology* 13:35-47.

Kaufmann, Merrill R.; Graham, Russell T.; Boyce, Douglas A. Jr; and others. 1994. *An Ecological Basis for Ecosystem Management.* General Technical Report RM-246. Fort Collins, CO: U.S. Department of Agriculture, Forest Service, Rocky Mountain Forest and Range Experiment Station. 22p.

Kaufmann, Merrill R.; Moir, W.H.; Bassett, Richard L., technical coordinators. 1992. *Old-Growth Forests in the Southwest and Rocky Mountain Regions: Proceedings of a Workshop.* 1992 March 9-13, Portal, AZ. General Technical Report RM-213. Fort Collins, CO: U.S. Department of Agriculture, Forest Service, Rocky Mountain Forest and Range Experiment Station. 200 p.

Landis, Thomas D.; Tinus, Richard W.; McDonald, Stephen E.; Barnett, James P. Various years. *The Container Tree Nursery Manual.* Agriculture Handbook 674. Washington, DC: U.S. Department of Agriculture, Forest Service.

    Vol. 1 Container nursery planning, development, and management. 1995.

    Vol. 2 Containers and growing media. 1990.

    Vol. 3 Container nursery environment. 1992.

    Vol. 4 Seedling nutrition and irrigation. 1989.

    Vol. 5 The biological component: nursery pests and mycorrhizae. 1990.

    Vol. 6 Seedling propagation. 1999.

Lundquist, J.E. 1995. *Characterizing Disturbance in Managed Ponderosa Pine Stands in the Black Hills. Forest Ecology and Management* 74:61-74.

Mowrer, H. Todd, technical compiler. 1997. *Decision Support Systems for Ecosystem Management: an Evaluation of Existing Systems.* General Technical Report RM-GTR-296. Fort Collins, CO: U.S. Department of Agriculture, Forest Service, Rocky Mountain Forest and Range Experiment Station. 154 p.

Musselman, R. C., technical coordinator. 1992. *The Glacier Lakes Ecosystem Experiments Site.* General Technical Report RM-249. Fort Collins, CO: U.S. Department of Agriculture, Forest Service, Rocky Mountain Forest and Range Experiment Station. 94 p.

Perla, Ronald I.; Martinelli, M. Jr. 1976. *Avalanche Handbook.* Agriculture Handbook 489. Washington, D.C.: U.S. Department of Agriculture, Forest Service. 238 p

Peterson, George L.; Driver, Beverly S.; Gregory, Robin (editors). 1988. *Public Amenity Resource Valuation: Integrating Economics With Other Disciplines.* University Park, PA: Venture Press. 260 p.

Peterson, George S.; McCollum, Daniel W.; Swanson, Cindy S.; Thomas, Michael. 1992. *Valuing Wildlife Resources in Alaska.* Boulder, CO: Westview Press. 357 p.

Price, Raymond. 1976. *History of Forest Service Research in the Central and Southern Rocky Mountain Regions, 1908   1975.* General Technical Report RM-27. Fort Collins, CO: U.S. Department of Agriculture, Forest Service, Rocky Mountain Forest and Range Experiment Station. 100 p. (Available on the web at: http://www.fs.fed.us/rm/pubs rm/rm gtr027.html)

Reynolds, Richard T.; Graham, Russell T.; Reiser, M. Hildegard; and others. 1992. *Management Recommendations for the Northern Goshawk in the Southwestern United States.* General Technical Report RM-217. Fort Collins, CO: U.S. Department of Agriculture, Forest Service, Rocky Mountain Forest and Range Experiment Station. 90 p.

Riffle, Jerry W.; Peterson, Glenn W. (technical coordinators). 1986. *Diseases of Trees in the Great Plains.* General Technical Report RM-129. Fort Collins, CO: U.S. Department of Agriculture, Forest Service, Rocky Mountain Forest and Range Experiment Station. 149 p.

Rinne, John N.; Minckley, W. L. 1991. *Native Fishes of Arid Lands: a Dwindling Resource in the Desert Southwest.* General Technical Report RM-206. Fort Collins, CO: U.S. Department of Agriculture, Forest Service, Rocky Mountain Forest and Range Experiment Station. 45 p.

Schmid, J.M.; Frye, R.H. 1977. *Spruce Beetle in Colorado.* General Technical Report RM-49. Fort Collins, CO: U.S. Department of Agriculture, Forest Service, Rocky Mountain Forest and Range Experiment Station. 38 p.

Schreuder, Hans T.; Gregoire, Timothy G.; Wood, Geoffrey B. 1993. *Sampling Methods for Multiresource Forest Inventory.* John Wiley & Sons, Inc. 446 p.

Shaw, Douglas W.; Finch, Deborah H., technical coordinators. 1996. *Desired Future Conditions for Southwestern Riparian Ecosystems: Bringing Interests and Concerns Together.* 1995 Sept. 18-22; Albuquerque, NM. General Technical Report RM-GTR-272. Fort Collins, CO: U.S. Department of Agriculture, Forest Service, Rocky Mountain Forest and Range Experiment Station. 395 p.

Shepperd, W. D.; Troendle, C. A.; Edminster, C. B. 1992. *Linking Water and Growth and Yield Models to Evaluate Management Alternatives in Subalpine Ecosystems.* Pp. 42-48. *In:* Getting to the future through silviculture. Proceedings of the National Silviculture Workshop. May 6-9, 1991. Cedar City, UT. General Technical Report INT-291. Ogden, UT: U.S. Department of Agriculture, Forest Service, Intermountain Forest and Range Experiment Station.

Sommerfeld, R. A.; Mosier, A. R.; Musselman, R. C. 1993. *CO2, CH4 and N2O Flux Through a Wyoming Snowpack and Implications for Global Budgets.* Nature. 361(6408): 140-142.

Stokes, Marvin A.: Dieterich, John H. (technical coordinators). 1980. *Proceedings of the Fire History Workshop.* General Technical Report RM-81. Fort Collins, CO: U.S. Department of Agriculture, Forest Service, Rocky Mountain Forest and Range Experiment Station. 142 p.

Tabler, R. D. 1994. *Design Guidelines for Control of Blowing and Drifting Snow.* SHRP-H-381. Strategic Highway Research Program, National Research Council. 364 p.

Tainter, Joseph A.; Hamre, R.H., editors. 1988. *Tools to Manage the Past: Research Priorities for Cultural Resources Management in the Southwest.* 1988 May 2-6, Grand Canyon, AZ. General Technical Report RM-164. Fort Collins, CO: U.S. Department of Agriculture, Forest Service, Rocky Mountain Forest and Range Experiment Station. 214 p.

Tellman, Barbara; Cortner, Hanna J.; Wallace, Mary G.; DeBano, Leonard F.; Hamre, R. H. (technical coordinators). 1993. *Riparian Management: Common Threads and Shared Interests.* General Technical Report RM-226. Fort Collins, CO: U.S. Department of Agriculture, Forest Service, Rocky Mountain Forest and Range Experiment Station. 419 p.

Tellman, Barbara; Finch, Deborah M.; Edminster, Carl; Hamre, Robert (editors). 1998. *The Future of Arid Grasslands: Identifying Issues, Seeking Solutions.* Proceedings RMRS-P-3. Fort Collins, CO: U.S. Department of Agriculture, Forest Service, Rocky Mountain Forest and Range Experiment Station. 392 p.

Troendle, Charles A.; Kaufmann, Merrill R.; Hamre, R. H.; Winokur, Robert P. (technical coordinators). 1987. *Management of Subalpine Forests: Building on 50 Years of Research.* Proceedings of a technical conference, July 5-7, Silver Creek, CO. General Technical Report RM-149. Fort Collins, CO: U.S. Department of Agriculture, Forest Service, Rocky Mountain Forest and Range Experiment Station. 253 p.

Troendle, Charles A.; King, Rudy M. 1987. *The Effect of Partial Cutting and Clearcutting on the Deadhorse Creek Watershed. Journal of Hydrology* 90: 145-157.

Uresk, Daniel W. 1990. *Using Multivariate Techniques to Quantitatively Estimate Ecological Stages in a Mixed Grass Prairie. Journal of Range Management* 43(4):282-285.

USDA Fish and Wildlife Service. 1955. *Recovery Plan for the Mexican Spotted Owl.* USDI Fish and Wildlife Service, Albuquerque, NM. 172 p.

Yoder, B. J.; Ryan, M. G.; Waring, R. H.; and others. 1994. *Evidence of Reduced Photosynthetic Rates in Old Trees. Forest Science.* 40(3)513-527.

Personnel at the Rocky Mountain Forest and Range Experiment Station, 1976-1997

A

Abt, Steve – FC
Acheson, Ann – FC
Adair, Clarence – FC
Adams, Judy – FC
Aguilar, Richard – Alb
Aitkin, J. Kevin – Tem
Aldon, Earl – Alb
Aldrich, Robert – FC
Alexander, Robert – FC
Alig, Ralph – FC
Allasia, David – FC
Allen, D. Neil – FC
Allen, Deborah – FC
Almaguer, Diane – FC
Altamirano, Nora – Alb
Alward, Gregory – FC
Ames, Sheila – FC
Amundson, Arlene – FC
Anderson, Jana – FC
Anderson, Mark – RC
Anderson, Michael – FC
Anderson, Patricia – Flag
Angel, Kathleen – Tem
Anglin, Willis – FC
Armstrong, Mary – Lar
Armstrong, Sally – RC

B

Bailey, Robert – FC
Baker, Malchus, Jr. – Flag
Baker, Sandra – Flag
Ball, Laurie – FC
Ballard, Sue – FC
Ballinger, Cynthia – FC
Balser, Janet – FC
Baltic, Tony – FC
Barkdoll, Donna – FC
Barney, Frances – FC
Barnhart, Michael – Lin
Barreth, Tracy – RC
Bartscher, Janet – RC
Bath, Norma – FC

Batt, Carin – FC
Bauer, Sue – FC
Baughman, Valerie – FC
Bayman, Nancy – FC
Beagle, Larry – RC
Beasom, Sam – Lub
Beaugh, Debra – FC
Bedan, Rebecca – FC
Belfit, Scott – Tem
Belish, Timberley – Lar
Bemis, Laura – FC
Bergen, James – FC
Bevers, B. Michael – FC
Bernhardt, Lee – FC
Blakey, Shari – FC
Block, William – Flag
Bird, Kenneth – Lar
Bjugstad, Ardell – RC
Blair, Glen – Tem
Block, William – Flag
Bloyd, Judith – FC
Boboricken, Sherry – FC
Boldt, Charles – RC
Booker, Melvin – FC
Bornong, Joanne – Lar
Bouldes, Charlene – FC
Bowden, Kenneth – FC
Bowman, Dale – Flag
Bowman, Sharon – FC
Boyce, Barbara – Flag
Boyd, Wilbert – FC
Bradley, John – Flag
Bradley, Linda – FC
Brady, Steve – FC
Brain, Janice – FC
Bratton, Gerald – Lin
Brink, Glen – FC
Brockway, Dale – Alb
Brown, Douglas – FC
Brown, Gary – Lar
Brown, Karen – FC
Brown, Thomas – FC
Bunker, Jean – FC
Burd, John – Lub

Burnett, Alan – Flag
Burns, Denver – FC
Burr, Karen – Flag
Burris, Victoria – FC
Butler, Norma – FC
Butler, Robert – Flag

C

Cable, Dwight – Tuc
Cables, Jacqueline – FC
Cade, Delloris – FC
Cain, Daria – FC
Campbell, Ralph – Flag
Carberry, Robert – FC
Carder, D. Ross – Flag
Carman, Dan – Lin
Carpenter, David – Flag
Carpenter, Henry – Lar
Carter, Deborah – FC
Casner, Wilson – Tem
Cefkin, Rose – FC
Chalk, David – FC
Chamberlain, Valden – Tem
Champ, Patricia – FC
Champagne, Norman – Flag
Chapman, Carl – FC
Chavez, M. Angela – FC
Christensen, Karla – Lar
Christensen, Sylvia – Lin
Chung, Lois – FC
Chung-McCoubrey, Alice – Alb
Clancy, Karen – Flag
Clark, Andrea – FC
Clausen, Dru – FC
Cocanour, Rebecca – FC
Cockrell, Kathy – RC
Cogar, Virginia – Tem
Coley, Harold – FC
Collins, Loa – FC
Collins, Vera – Lar
Comer, Sherilyn – FC
Connell, Bernadette – FC
Conrad, Mark – Lar

Cook-Obedzinsky, Connie – FC
Cooper, Sharon – Flag
Cottier, Jan – FC
Cottrell, Kimberly – Lin
Cox, Don – FC
Creg, Burt – Lin
Crenshaw, Toni – FC
Cress, William – Alb
Crouch, Glenn – FC
Crowley, Mary – Flag
Crutchfield, Marie – FC
Cunningham, Charles – FC
Curran, Ed – FC
Currie, Pat – FC
Czaplewski, Raymond – FC
Czech, Doris – Flag

D

D'Angelo, Bonnie – FC
Dailey, Mai – FC
Damon, Bernece – Flag
Dana, Robert – FC
Daniels, Joan – RC
Daron, Sally – FC
Davenport, Walt – FC
Davis, Edwin – Tem
Davis, Phyllis – FC
Davis, Vaughn – FC
Dean, Julie – FC
DeBano, Leonard – Tem
DeHerrera, Beverly – FC
Denison, Steve – RC
Dieterich, John – Tem
Dillon, Madelyn – FC
Dillon, Patricia – FC
DiSenso, Ann – FC
Dix, Mary Ellen – Lin
Dixon, Gary – FC
Dixon, Victoria – FC
Dixon, Willie – FC
Dodds, Margie – FC
Doherty, Erin – Lar
Dolanski, Sharon – FC
Donnelly, Dennis – FC
Donovan, Cheryl – FC
Donovan, Dennis – FC

Dosskey, Michael – Lin
Dotts, Hazel – FC
Dove, Deborah – FC
Driscoll, Richard – FC
Driver, Beverly – FC
Duidley, Sheralyn – FC
Durham, Marion – Flag
Duvall, Vinson – Tem
Dwyer, Jill – Flag

E

Eades, Chris
Earley, Denise – FC
Edminster, Carleton – Flag
Egeland, Leanne – FC
Ellison, Gail – Lin
Ellsworth, Alan – Lar
Eoff, Joan – FC
Erickson, Bernard – FC
Ertl, Mary – Flag
Eskew, Lane – FC
Evridge, Jenny – RC

F

Fager, Barbara – FC
Farlee, Janet – Lin
Farrar, Pamela – FC
Fasick, Clyde – FC
Feable, Lawrence – RC
Fedde, Kari – FC
Feddema, Charles – FC
Finch, Deborah – Alb
Fisher, Richard – FC
Fitch, Shirley – Flag
Flather, Curtis – FC
Fletcher, Charles (Rick) – FC
Fletcher, Tonya – FC
Flores, Deborah – FC
Forbs, Linda – Flag
Ford, Paulette – Alb
Fornwalt, Nevin – Lar
Fosberg, Michael – FC
Fox, Douglas – FC
Francis, Kerry – FC
Francis, Richard – Alb

Frank, Ernest – RC
Freeman, Duane – FC
Freeman, Lee – FC
Freeman, Linda – FC
Fresquez, Phillip – Alb
Funderhide, Emma – FC
Furman, R. William – FC

G

Galida, Cheryl – FC
Gallegos, Carmen – Alb
Gallup, Darrell – FC
Ganey, Joseph – Flag
Garcia, Diana – FC
Garcia, George – Alb
GarciaSanchez, Elizabeth – Alb
Garrett, Lawrence – Flag
Gary, Barbara – FC
Gary, Howard – FC
Gasperetti, Sheila – FC
Gatz, William – FC
Geary, Joann – FC
Geils, Brian – Flag
Gilbert, Bonnie – FC
Gilbert, Mary – Tem
Gilbert, Michael – FC
Gilmore, Becky – FC
Girard, Michele – RC
Girard, Van – FC
Glass, Kathy – FC
Gomez, Josephine – Tem
Gonzales, Manuel – Alb
Good, Mary – FC
Goodwin, Gregory – Lar
Gorman, Susan – Alb
Gottfried, Gerald – Flag
Greentree, Wallace – FC
Greenwald, Emilie – FC
Griego, Rudy – Tem
Grubb, Teryl – Flag
Gurley-Davis, Karen – Flag
Gutierrez, Rudy – FC
Gutzwiller, Pamela – Lar

H

Haase, Sally – Tem
Hager, Judy – FC
Hager, Victor – FC
Hagihara, James – FC
Halvorsen, Marsha – FC
Hamre, Robert – FC
Hansen, Sigrid – FC
Hanson, Esther – FC
Harrington, Michael – Tem
Harris, Barbara – FC
Harris, Margaret – FC
Harrison, Anne – FC
Hart, Joyce – FC
Hart, Steve – FC
Hart, Timothy – FC
Haskell, Jim – FC
Hastings, Evelyn – Flag
Hawkes, Clifford – RC
Hawksworth, Frank – FC
Hayes, Deborah – Alb
Hayes, Pamela – FC
Haynes, Richard – FC
Hayward, Gregory – Lar
Heede, Burchard – Tem
Hegg, Karl – FC
Hehn, Theodore – FC
Heidmann, LeRoy – Flag
Heidrich, Mary – Alb
Henry, Hank – Lar
Henry, Stephen – Lar
Hernandez, Xavier – Tem
Herrick, David – FC
Hiatt, Harvey – Flag
Hibbert, Alden – Tem
Hinds, Thomas – FC
Hirsch, Stanley – FC
Hittner, Virginia – Lin
Hodorff, Robert – Lar
Hoek, Roger – FC
Hoekstra, Sharon – FC
Hoekstra, Thomas – FC
Hof, John – FC
Holland, Eric – Tem
Holub, E. William – FC
Hooten, Vicki – Lub

Horton, Bonita – Lub
Horton, Jerry – FC
Hovland, Teddy – Lin
Hubbard, Robert – FC
Huebner, Daniel – Flag
Huerta, Deborah – FC
Hulbert, Frank – FC
Humphries, Hope – FC
Huntsberger, Janine – Flag
Huwa, Daryl – Bot

I

Ippolito, Kelly – FC
Irwin, Jennifer – Lin
Irwin, Kris – Lin
Isaacson, Kim – Lin

J

Jacob-Mua, Joyce – Lin
Jacobs, Debbie – FC
Jacobs, Joyce – Lin
Jairell, Robert – Lar
Jakle, Martin – Tem
James, Marsha – FC
Jameson, Donald – FC
Janzen, Susan – FC
Javersak, Jody – RC
Jeffrey, Katherine – FC
Jemison, Roy – Alb
Jenkins, Philip – Tem
Jensen, Debra – FC
Johnson, Curtis – Flag
Johnson, Philip – FC
Joy, Suzanne – FC
Joyce, Linda – FC
Judson, Arthur – FC

K

Karnuth, Leif – Alb
Kaufmann, Merrill – FC
Kaulitz, Zita – RC
Keefer, Donald – FC
Kehr, Harold – FC
Kelley, Donald – RC

Kelley, Margaret – FC
Kelly, Lorraine – Lar
Kelly, Jeff – Alb
Kennedy, Sharyce – RC
Kent, Brian – FC
Kent, Judy – Tem
Kerbs, Roger – FC
Kidneigh, Connie – FC
Killoran, Kathryn – Bot
Kimbrough, David – FC
King, Rudy – FC
Klein, David – FC
Kleinschmit, Sarah – RC
Klopatek, Carole – Flag
Klopfenstein, Ned – Lin
Knaub, Judy – FC
Knipe, Oren – Tem
Knott, F. William – FC
Knutson, Tonya – FC
Kovner, Jacob – FC
Krammes, J. Sam – FC
Krebill, Richard – Tem
Kress, Marsha – FC
Krug, Virginia – FC
Kruse, William – Flag
Kuharski, Kathy – FC
Kuhl, Michael – Lin
Kulongowski, Barbara – Tem
Kunis, Daniel – FC

L

LaBau, V. James – FC
Lance, Barbara – Tem
Lane, Mark – Tem
Laird, Kay – FC
Larson, Frederic – Flag
Laskowski, Peggy – Lar
Latterell, Dolores – FC
Layman, Robert – Flag
Leaf, Jennifer – FC
Lee, Susan – FC
Leibbrandt, Luann – FC
Lemieux, April – FC
Lewis, Gordon – FC
Lewis, Nancy – Tem
Lightfoot, Frank – Flag

Lindeborg, Richard – FC
Litten, Carol – FC
Litten, Sharon – FC
Lizarraga, Alicia – FC
Loftin, Sam – Alb
Lopez, Jamelyn – FC
Lopez, Roy – Flag
Loring, Michael – RC
Loveless, Charles – FC
Lozano, Fay – Flag
Lucero, August – Alb
Luffman, Tina – Flag
Lukens, Don – FC
Lukoic, Jacquelyn – FC
Lumar, Carolyn – FC
Lund, H. Gyde – FC
Lundquist, John – FC
Lynch, Ann – Flag

M

MacDonald, Patricia – FC
Manley, LeRoy – FC
Manthos, Barbara – FC
Markstrom, Donald – FC
Marsden, Michael – FC
Marsh, Linda – FC
Martin, S. Clark – Tuc
Martin, Vicki – FC
Martinelli, Mario – FC
Martinez, Dorothy – FC
Martinez, Manuel – FC
Martinez, Raymond – FC
Martischang, Martin – Tem
Massey, Barbara – Flag
Massman, William – FC
Mata, Stephen – FC
Mattingly, Christine – FC
Mattson, Julie – Lar
McCallum, James – FC
McCambridge, William – FC
McCartney, Catherine – FC
McCollum, Daniel – FC
McConnell, Jerry – Flag
McCormick, Dean – FC
McCoy, R. Diane – FC
McCutchan, Morris – FC

McDonald, Stephen – FC
McDonnell, Susan – FC
McElderry, Sue – FC
McElvain, William – Tem
McGuire, Patricia – FC
McGuire, Richard – FC
McKinney, William – FC
McLendon, Judy – FC
McNutt, Betty – Tem
Means, Margarite – FC
Means, Michael – Alb
Medina, Alvin – Flag
Melendrez, Valentine – FC
Mehl, Garnet – FC
Meisinger, Doris – FC
Meisinger, Lynnette – FC
Merkel, Daniel – FC
Merrill, Laura – FC
Merritt, Norman – FC
Messner, Harold – RC
Meyer, Joni – RC
Michel, Pat – FC
Millard, Ann – FC
Miller, LindaLu – FC
Mills, Thomas – FC
Miranda, Fernando – FC
Mitchell, James – Flag
Mitchell, John – FC
Mitchell, Joseph – FC
Moir, William – Flag
Montrey, Henry – FC
Moore, Darleen – FC
Mora, Karen – FC
Morris, Karen – FC
Morris, Meredith – FC
Mossburg, Glynndora – FC
Mowrer, H. Todd – FC
Muchow, Linda – FC
Muecke, Nancy – Tem
Mulcahy, Patti – FC
Muniz, Shirley – FC
Murray, Marjorie – FC
Musselman, Robert – FC
Myhre, Richard – FC

N

Nankervis, James – FC
Neary, Daniel – Flag
Neeld, Vaughn – FC
Nelson, Brytten – Flag
Negron, Jose – FC
Neubauer, Lucille – Bot
Nevarez, Elizabeth – Alb
Nichols, Winnie – FC
Nickerson, Mona – FC
Nightingale, Monty – Flag
Noble, Daniel – RC
Norris, DeDe – FC
North, William – FC
Nungesser, Martha – FC
Nuvamsa, Benjamin – Flag

O

Obedzinski, Robert – FC
O'Connell, Beverly – FC
O'Deen, Louise – FC
O'Doherty, Erin – Lar
O'Keefe, Judy – FC
Oglesby, Carla – FC
Oler, Eleanor – Lin
Olsen, William – FC
Omeg, Karen – FC
Omdal, Daniel – FC
Organo, Martha – FC
Orr, Howard – RC
Ortmann, Kristeen – FC
Overby, Steven – Flag
Owens, Janet – FC
Ozment, Arnold – Tem

P

Padilla, Charles – FC
Padilla, Mary – FC
Parchman, Marguerite – FC
Parker, Lloyd – FC
Parrish, Kelly – FC
Parrish, Tracy – FC
Parsons, Linda – RC
Pase, Charles – Alb

Pasek, Judy – Lin
Patterson, Joyce – FC
Pattison, Jennifer – Alb
Patton, David – Tem
Patton-Mallory, Marcia – FC
Paulsen, Harold – FC
Periman, Richard – Alb
Perotin, Beverly – FC
Perry, Hazel – Tem
Perry, Judy – FC
Peters, Debbie – FC
Petersen, Louis – FC
Petersen, Lynnette – FC
Peterson, George – FC
Peterson, Glenn – Lin
Pettigrew, Sharon – Flag
Pforr, Martha – FC
Pierson, Virginia – Lin
Pinther, Linda – FC
Piotter, Laura – FC
Pippett, Kerwin – Tem
Pomeroy, John – Lar
Pope, V. Fay – FC
Porth, Laurie – FC
Pott, Alfred – Flag
Potyondy, John – FC
Prince, N. Diane – Flag
Prine, Virginia – FC
Prosser, Joseph – Flag
Pursley, Barbara – FC

Q
Qualls, Debra – FC

R
Rader, Russell – Lar
Radloff, David – FC
Rafsnider, Giles – FC
Raish, Carol – Alb
Range, Patricia – FC
Raphael, Martin – Lar
Ray, Marsha – FC
Read, Ralph – Lin
Redden, Terry – FC
Regan, Claudia – FC

Reichert, Don – FC
Reid, Janie – FC
Reynolds, Richard – FC
Rietveld, Willis – Lin
Riffle, Jerry – Lin
Rinne, John – Flag
Ritterhouse, Patricia – FC
Rivera, Shannon – FC
Roberts, David – Tem
Roberts, Edwin – FC
Rochelle, Shannon – FC
Rodgers, Lonnie – FC
Rogers, James – Tem
Ronco, Frank – Flag
Ronne, Ruth – Lin
Rosenthal, Donald – FC
Ross, Kim – Flag
Ross, Sharon – FC
Roth-Tucker, Karen – FC
Roussopoulos, Peter – FC
Ruble, Angela – FC
Rudzek, Vickie – FC
Ruggiero, Leonard – Lar
Rumble, Mark – RC
Russo, Katherine – FC
Rutledge, Carolyn – FC
Ryan, Joseph – Tem
Ryan, Michael – FC
Ryan-Burkett, Sandra – Lar

S
Sackett, Stephen – Flag
Sagmeister, Renay – FC
Salas, Anthony – FC
Sampson, George – FC
Sanchez, Henry – Flag
Sanders, Deborah – FC
Sanderson, Darlene – FC
Sandoval, Larry – FC
Sawell, Laniece – RC
Schanhols, Sue – FC
Schenderline, Inez – FC
Schmid, John – FC
Schmidt, Larry – FC
Schmidt, Ralph – FC
Schneider, Richard – FC

Schoeneberger, Michele – Lin
Schoettle, Anna – FC
Schofield, Debra – FC
Scholl, David – Alb
Schopfer, Walter – FC
Schreuder, Hans – FC
Schubert, Gilbert – Flag
Schultz, Yvonne – Bot
Schumann, Carol – Lin
Schwab, Caroline – FC
Schweitzer, Dennis – FC
Scott, Jeffrey – FC
Scritchfield, William – FC
Seaver, Rhonda – RC
Seaworth, Sharon – FC
Seltzer, Amy – Lin
Senn, Sara – FC
Serrano, Lynette – FC
Severson, Kieth – Tem
Shallman, James – Flag
Shaw, Charles – FC
Shefferd, Jessie – FC
Shelton, Clover – Lin
Shepperd, Wayne – FC
Shields, Deborah – FC
Short, Henry – Tem
Shriver, D. Jane – Lar
Sieg, Carolyn – RC
Sieverding, Rebecca – FC
Simpson, Deborah – FC
Sims, Jeffrey – Flag
Smika, Jennifer – FC
Smith, Bobbie – FC
Smith, Dixie – FC
Smith, Dwain – FC
Smith, Ernest – Tem
Smith, Harold – Tem
Snow, Jerry – Flag
Snyder, Caroline – Tem
Solomon, Alberta – FC
Sommerfeld, Richard – FC
Sorg, Cindy – FC
Spaulding, Judy – Flag
Sprackling, John – FC
Sprenger, Terry – FC
Squires, John – Lar
Staley, John – FC

Steed, James – Flag
Stevens, Robert – FC
Stevenson, Orvil – Flag
Stormer, Fred – FC
Stottlemeyer, Robert – FC
Straw, Judy – Lar
Straus, Patricia – FC
Streedbeck, Janet – Lin
Strohmeyer, Brenda – Flag
Stuart, Kirsten – Lin
Sturges, David – Lar
Swanson, Cindy – FC
Swanson, Marjorie – FC
Szaro, Robert – Tem

T

Tabler, Ronald – Lar
Tackle, David – FC
Tagestad, Arden – Bot
Tapia, Esteban – FC
Tainter, Joe – Alb
Telles, Lorenzo – Flag
Tewa, Fermina – FC
Tharalson, Teresa – Tem
Thilenius, John – Lar
Thomas, Mary – Alb
Thompson, Debra – FC
Thompson, Jesse – FC
Thornton, Jana – FC
Tidwell, Ted – FC
Tinus, Richard – Flag
Traywick, Rose – RC
Troendle, Charles – FC
Trowbridge, Nora – FC
Trujillo, David – Flag
Turnbull, Gene – FC
Turner, Gladys – FC
Twito, Tina – FC

U

Uresk, Daniel – RC

V

Vahle, Robert – Tem
Valenzuela, Elias – Flag
Van Deusen, James – RC
Van Deusen, Larry – FC
Van Glarik, Janet – FC
Van Haverbeke, David – Lin
Vertucci, Frank – FC
Vigil, Deborah – FC
Voorhees, Marguerite – FC

W

Wagg, Helen – FC
Wager, Tracy – FC
Waite, Audrey – Tem
Waity, Charla – FC
Walker, Leon – FC
Walker, Sheila – FC
Waltermire, Karel – FC
Ward, A. Lorin – Lar
Ward, Pat – Flag
Watkins, Ross – FC
Weis, Eleanor (Hamre) – FC
Werth, Lee – FC
West, A. Viola – FC
West, Linda – FC
West, Phyllis – Tem
Wester, Ronald – FC
Weymouth, Richard – FC
Wheatley, George – FC
Wheeler, Jean – FC
Whelan, James – FC
White, P. Wayne – FC
Whitfield, Marilyn – FC
Whitedove, Meria – FC
Whiteman, Brenda – Flag
Whitney, Donice – FC
Whitney, Rachel – FC
Wicker, Ed – FC
Wight, Bruce – Lin
Wiley, Ardath – FC
Williams, Jill – FC
Williams, Knox – FC
Williams, Leon – FC
Williams, Michael – FC

Williams, Penny – FC
Williams, Tod – Alb
Wilson, Virginia – FC
Winder, Carol – FC
Wingstrom, Betty – FC
Winokur, Robert – FC
Winter, Charles – Lar
Wittenauer, Paula – FC
Wolf, Mona – FC
Wolfe, Frank – FC
Wolfe, Marvin – FC
Wolters, Gale – Alb
Wood, Diane – Flag
Wood, Sarah – Alb
Wooten, Sharon – FC
Workman, Sarah – Lin
Worth, Harold – FC

Y

Yamamoto, Teruo – RC
Yancik, Richard – FC
Yarrington, Charlotte – FC
Yockey, Carol – FC
Yontz, Mavis – FC
Young, Michael – Lar

Z

Zegar, Marie – FC
Zeller, Karl – FC

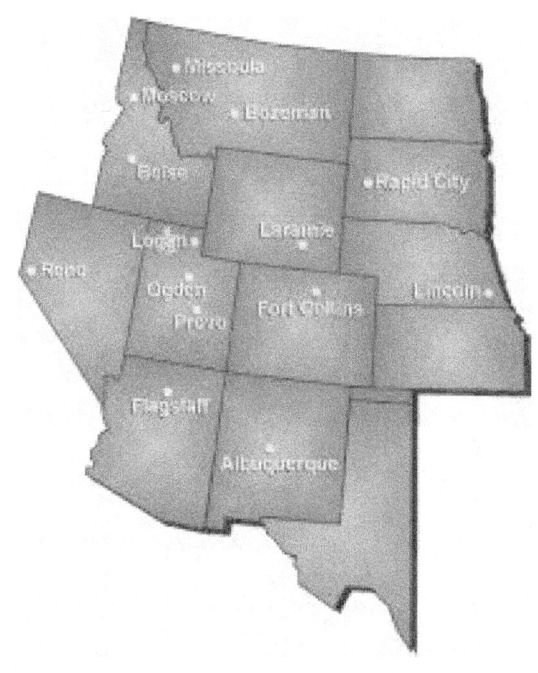

www.ingramcontent.com/pod-product-compliance
Lightning Source LLC
Chambersburg PA
CBHW080523290526
45790CB00006B/2282